Reading the Bible Wisely

Reading the Bible Wisely

An Introduction to Taking Scripture Seriously
Revised Edition

RICHARD S. BRIGGS

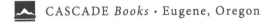 CASCADE *Books* · Eugene, Oregon

READING THE BIBLE WISELY
An Introduction to Taking Scripture Seriously
Revised edition

Cascade Books
An Imprint of Wipf and Stock Publishers
199 W. 8th Ave., Suite 3
Eugene, OR 97401

www.wipfandstock.com

ISBN 13: 978-1-61097-288-8

This book is a revised and expanded edition of Richard S. Briggs, *Reading the Bible Wisely*. London: SPCK; and Grand Rapids: Baker Academic, 2003.

New Revised Standard Version Bible, copyright 1989, Division of Christian Education of the National Council of the Churches of Christ in the United States of America. Used by permission. All rights reserved.

Cataloging-in-Publication data:

Briggs, Richard, 1966–

Reading the Bible wisely : an introduction to taking scripture seriously. revised edition / Richard S. Briggs.

p. ; cm. — Includes bibliographical references and index.

ISBN 13: 978-1-61097-288-8

1. Bible—Hermeneutics. I. Title.

BS476 B615 2011

Manufactured in the U.S.A.

To Joshua
who has helped me to see many things,
including the Bible,
with opened eyes

Contents

Preface to the Revised Edition

READING THE BIBLE WISELY was first published in the UK by SPCK, and in the USA by Baker Academic, in 2003. It was always intended as a short *introduction* to the task—not comprehensive, not overwhelming, not unduly partisan. Although now I am very much aware of so many other things one could say, and so many other approaches to consider, I think it fulfilled a useful function of saying a limited number of things clearly. In particular, it reflected my conviction that we should let scripture itself shape our thinking about how we handle scripture.

In revising the book I have tried to keep its introductory nature in mind and not overwhelm the text with reference to the many things I have thought or read since. It is now clear that this modest offering was an early attempt to articulate what might today be called "theological interpretation." I did not write it in 2003 with that phrase in mind, but it now seems an appropriate label for what is done here.

On one point I have come to realize the need for considerably greater nuance. Around the time the first edition was published I moved from a job teaching the New Testament to my present position where I teach the Old Testament. At the last minute I had added a line to the book to acknowledge the fact that all my examples, and indeed most of my thinking, were taken from the New Testament. Confidently I proclaimed, "That it is the New Testament which is mainly in view was not for any profound or theological reason: I just happen to be more familiar with seeing how hermeneutical issues arise out of it than with the Old Testament, but in principle much of what follows could be re-expressed to show how it works with the Old Testament too." As I settled into my new role of teaching the Old Testament I came to see how inadequate such a statement was and is. Yes, in some ways, the issues are comparable. But in quite significant ways, the challenge of reading the Old Testament requires hermeneutical moves which the New Testament does not need. A second context is already built into Old Testament texts by virtue of their reappropriation into Christian scripture. One thing this clarifies is that I am writing here for Christians. Another is that the links between Jewish and Christian interpretation are complex and tremendously enriching. Were I to write the book from scratch, as it were, this two-testament structure of the Christian Bible would probably be a significant organizing feature of the discussion. Instead I have settled for a more modest revision, achieved by adding two chapters on the Old Testament, and revising many of the ways in which particular points were expressed (notably about the development of the canon).

I have thoroughly edited the whole text for matters regarding clarity, awareness of Old Testament perspectives, and so forth. For this revision I have removed some errors as well as digressions, which I now think did not aid the book's purpose, including a chapter from the original on "the difficulty of scripture." Finally, I have added versions of a couple of pieces I have written more recently on the transformative potential of scripture.

The result is a new book, which is in some ways the same as the old book, and in other ways a new creation: a pleasing mixture of continuity and discontinuity from my current perspective as a Christian teaching the Old Testament.

Richard Briggs
Maundy Thursday
April 2011

Acknowledgments

IT IS A DELIGHT to see this book obtain a new lease of life through the encouragement, care, and attention of all at Cascade Books, an imprint of Wipf and Stock Publishers. In addition to continued thanks to Alison Barr and Richard Harvey for their assistance and enthusiasm with the first edition, I am much indebted to Chris Spinks for wisdom and encouragement in bringing about this revision.

Chapters 4 and 5 of this revised edition are both adapted from work previously published by Grove Books, based in Cambridge, England. My thinking about the Old Testament has been helpfully shaped by participation in their wonderful editorial team for biblical studies, and I am grateful to Ian Paul for permission to adapt and reproduce here material tried out first in my *Why Read the Old Testament?* and *Reading Isaiah. A Beginner's Guide*. Details of these and other of my publications for Grove may be found online at http://www.grovebooks.co.uk. Chapters 10 and 11 are both adapted (and in the latter case considerably shortened) from articles originally published in the UK Anglican journal *Anvil*. For the longer versions see respectively "Getting Involved: Speech Acts and Biblical Interpretation" and "The Role of the Bible in Formation and Transformation: A Hermeneutical and Theological Analysis." I would like to thank Andrew Goddard, editor of *Anvil*, for permission to make use of this material here.

Abbreviations

COS	W. W. Hallo and K. L. Younger, eds., *The Context of Scripture*. 3 vols. Leiden: Brill, 1997–2002.
KJV	King James Version
LXX	Septuagint
NEB	New English Bible
NIV	New International Version
NRSV	New Revised Standard Version
REB	Revised English Bible
//	Parallel passage

Introduction

WHAT DOES IT MEAN to read the Bible wisely? How do we take scripture seriously? This book offers some ways of beginning to answer these questions. We will be considering both how to interpret the Bible and how to think about the Bible.

Bible readers often, in my view, get sidetracked by some related but rather different questions: How can we know whether our interpretation is right? Can we be sure that the biblical text in front of us could not mean something else? I am not sure that such assurance is available in general, and I do not intend to try and offer it in what follows. Perhaps the biblical text can mean a rather wide range of things. It certainly seems to be taken in a wide range of ways in both church and academy, and there is no sign at present that we will soon all start to agree with each other on questions of interpretation.

Does it all depend on what we are looking for? I once had a student answer an exam question that required him to comment on points of interest in the opening chapters of Job. He came to Job 2:9, which contains the startling report that "his wife said to him, 'Do you still persist in your integrity? Curse God and die.'" There is quite a lot worth commenting on in that verse, from all sorts of angles. He wrote: "From this verse we can tell that Job had a wife." This may be an extreme case of a lack of inquisitiveness about the text, but it does illustrate that what people see in the Bible may depend on what they are looking for.

Whether the biblical text *can* mean whatever we might think it means is not the point. What it *can* mean often tells us more about ourselves than about the text. What it *does in practice* mean is the issue I want to address. What makes for an appropriate way to read the Bible? Put differently: What is the goal of Bible reading? Why read the Bible?

My observation is that most people who start to read the Bible do so for one or both of two reasons: it will tell them about God, and/ or it will help them understand how to live. This is certainly a fair way to begin, although as we will see in a later chapter there are in fact many further helpful answers to this question. But experience suggests that there are two further questions that soon occur to the beginning reader: How *should* we read the Bible? What should we think *about* the Bible? At this point a variety of things can happen, as we begin to reflect on our reading a little. This book is designed to help with that process of reflection.

In writing this book I have assumed that the reader is interested in reading the Bible, has perhaps read quite a lot of it, heard it preached frequently, and would tend to agree that—at least in some general way—Bible reading is good both for knowing God and for knowing how to live. But such a reader is also becoming aware that the Bible is interpreted in a variety of ways, many of them mutually contradictory. Arguments about the Bible, about its nature, and about how to interpret it can be among the most bitter and divisive that Christians generally experience, right along with arguments about worship styles and changing anything at church.

There are a couple of ways ahead for such a reader. First they can learn about "hermeneutics." Hermeneutics is the art (or science) of interpretation. If we are talking about the Bible then it is of course biblical interpretation that is in view. More generally "hermeneutics" is also the process of thinking about and evaluating biblical interpretations—moving up a level from reading a text this way or that way, and going on to ask questions about how to judge between competing interpretations. The first part of this book is a beginner's guide to some key aspects of hermeneutics. However, rather than talk hermeneutical theory, I have tried to introduce the theory by focusing on particular biblical passages and showing what sorts of questions about interpretation they raise. Hermeneutical thinking is one essential part of the skills and tools necessary to develop practices of good Bible reading.

Secondly, they can begin to think about what sort of book the Bible is. This is less a hermeneutical task—although it will always have hermeneutical elements—and more of a theological one. It is the construction of what is normally called a "doctrine of scripture." This too is a key aspect of cultivating good Bible reading. One problem is that it is often done in relative isolation from the first, hermeneutical, task. We start to talk about the Bible as, in some sense, the Word of God, or at the very least as the book that God wants us to read. If we are not careful, we may find ourselves handling the Bible in almost a "pre-hermeneutical" way as we pick out verses that prove this or that view of biblical authority or inspiration, or whatever our chosen topic is. In the second part of this book, therefore, I start to focus on these "doctrinal" questions. Again I try to let a study of various biblical passages show how the doctrines arise from reflecting upon the biblical text that we study.

The linking of these two different approaches is a complicated matter. It is not helped by the trend of academic specialization, which tends to mean that those who write books on hermeneutics are often not talking about the doctrine of scripture, and vice versa. On a simple introductory level, it is still common to find introductions to biblical interpretation which talk about how to interpret lots of different styles (genres) of biblical writing, or which look at how to find out what an author wanted to say, but do not address key theological points. They do not ask what difference it makes that the book we are looking at is the Bible. In theory it could be true that the Bible could be interpreted like any other book. In some limited ways this evidently is true, for example, regarding the importance of how to understand grammatical constructions, the features of poetry, sentence construction, and so forth. But it seems more likely that the uniqueness of the Bible requires some ways of interpreting it that are in fact unique.

More to the point, we need ways of thinking about the Bible which explicitly hold together the hermeneutical and the doctrinal approaches. What is the poor Bible reader, let alone pastor or preacher, to make of this split between "biblical studies" and "theology"? The biblical scholar may teach us that 1 Corinthians is part of Paul's correspondence with a church in Corinth in the mid-50s of the first century, and that we have to read it "contextually," in other words, aware of how Paul is adapting his words to his local context. The theologian might direct us to particular verses in 1 Corinthians and deduce all sorts of theological propositions, ranging from whether women are to be silent in church right through to views on subjects such as idolatry, homosexuality, or the resurrection—all of which get mentioned in 1 Corinthians. It sometimes feels as if the two approaches, and the two scholars, are simply not talking to each other.

One conviction underlying this book is that hermeneutics and doctrine need not be opposed in helping us to read well. What follows is intended as an exercise in leading the reader into some of the specific issues that arise when reading the Bible. These are issues that arise not out of the sheer ingenuity of the reader looking for something novel to talk about, but out of the text itself. In particular, they emerge out of the details and the specifics of the text as those details relate to the big (theological) picture.

The study of both hermeneutics and Christian doctrine is notoriously jargon-laden. I have tried to avoid as much jargon as I can. When I have needed a technical term I have tried both to show why it is needed and to define it clearly. In wanting to base the discussion on the details of the biblical text I occasionally need to talk about Hebrew or Greek details of that text, but the aim of doing this is simply to show why a certain issue is raised in a certain way. No knowledge of these languages is assumed. I have in general chosen the road less footnoted. It would not have been difficult to double or triple the number of notes, but it would also not have helped the reader who is just beginning to start grappling with these issues. This is an introductory book. If it does its job well then you will want to go on and read more thorough treatments after finishing this one.[1]

Part One of the book, then, explores hermeneutical issues to do with reading the Bible in an appropriate context. What kind of context could that be? I illustrate some of the possibilities with a focus, in the first instance, on the story of Jesus as found in the New Testament.

One key to wise reading may be historical context: Jesus' ministry on earth occupied a certain historical period and many of its details will remain obscure to us if we are not willing to invest in understanding the era on its own terms. Some would go further: not just the details but even the reasons behind Jesus' ministry must remain obscure to us if we do not grasp this time period in all its particular detail.

Another key may be literary context. What sort of writing is a gospel? Is it like a biography, or a modern history book, or a work of

---

1. The interested reader might turn to Fowl, *Theological Interpretation*, which includes many suggestions for further reading; and the two excellent collections of essays arising out of the interdisciplinary "Scripture Project" which ran for several years at Princeton: Davis and Hays, eds., *Art of Reading Scripture*; and Hays and Gaventa, eds., *Seeking Jesus*.

theology? How do we interpret stories Jesus told, or accounts of acts that he performed? What sorts of texts were the biblical authors writing?

A third sort of key may be a theological context. What makes a written account of Jesus different from, say, a written account of a Roman emperor of the time? We talk of miracles in the Gospel accounts: What makes them different from any other mighty acts performed at the time of Jesus? What makes Jesus' parables theologically different from the other parables told at the time? Why, fundamentally, does the New Testament carry that title: "New" in what sense? What does "testament" mean? We may say straightaway that it means "covenant," but what does it mean to say that the New Testament is a "new covenant"?

The understanding of these three different types of context, which inevitably overlap in various ways, occupies the first three chapters, as well as recurring in various places later on. The Gospel of Luke turns out to provide us with clear examples for all these three overlapping perspectives. A chapter on the Old Testament then considers some of the ways in which the issues do or do not differ as compared to the New Testament. The book of Isaiah allows us some illustrative examples of how the historical, literary and theological angles might look in the reading of some Old Testament texts.

In Part Two, we turn to consider specific doctrines about the Bible: its inspiration, its authority, and the significance of the "canon" of its writings. We ask what it means in practice to read the Bible as an inspired text, or as an authoritative text, and what it might mean to talk about "applying the Bible" today. Again, I attempt to show how these ideas relate to the reading of actual Bible passages.

Throughout, my conviction is that what we are looking for is an approach to the Bible which captures the essence of *wisdom*: a way to read the Bible wisely. Wisdom has not always been a heavily valued idea in our modern and/or postmodern world. We value choice, originality, interest, sincerity, therapy, even profit and success, and the Christian world is not short of books mirroring just these values: quick-fix "how to" books on church, prayer, relationships, and indeed on how to read the Bible.

But for the Christian, Bible reading is a spiritual discipline, both like and unlike any other. Like any spiritual discipline it requires maturity and wisdom, as well as a reading context of other Christians to support and challenge us. At the same time it is not like any other discipline, since it has its own technical requirements with which most of us are not so familiar. In Part Three of the book, I turn to some broader hermeneutical perspectives on how we might read scripture, with a particular focus on its transformative potential. Perhaps surprisingly, the book of Revelation serves as an initial New Testament focus for this discussion. Despite its reputation as a forbidding and complex book accessible only to fanatics and experts, the basic perspective of the book of Revelation offers a helpful way of understanding the importance of perspective and theological "eyes to see" as we read. Part Three then goes on to include some more general reflection on the kind of transformative effect on the reader which Bible reading can have.

As this final section suggests, and as the emphasis on wisdom indicates too, our goal throughout is to learn to read the Bible with open eyes. But the gift of eyes to see is a gift that only God can give, a point that we consider in the final chapter. If we are in any sense reading the Bible in order to know God, then that is precisely the way it should be.

Reading the Bible

1

Christian Scripture

The Road to Emmaus

LUKE 24:13–35

T HE EMMAUS STORY IS something of a classic for allowing us to focus on issues of biblical interpretation. The reasons will become clear as we follow the two disciples along the road. The journey takes us out from Jerusalem in a northwesterly direction towards Emmaus, although the "sixty stadia" given as the distance, roughly seven miles, appears to put us some considerable way beyond the probable site of Emmaus, an early indication that the road to biblical interpretation is rarely straightforward.

The passage starts "on that same day": the day that the women and the apostles have arrived at the empty tomb, puzzled and amazed. Two of them are walking along, one of whom is named in verse 18 as Cleopas. The other is unnamed, perhaps Luke himself, modestly hiding his identity rather as John does in the Fourth Gospel. Or perhaps it is Cleopas' wife, and thus they are a couple about to have their eyes opened rather as the first couple, Adam and Eve, did, only with a very different result. Perhaps we just do not know who Cleopas' companion is, which seems most likely, and is a gentle reminder that the pursuit of detail is not always fruitful.

They are joined on the road by a third companion, "but their eyes were kept from recognizing him" (v. 16). This surely does not mean that they could not spot the likeness, as if they were haunted by a vague feeling that they had seen him somewhere before, but just could not quite remember where. Luke does not elaborate, or say who it is that keeps them from recognizing. However, perhaps the text invites us to assume that this is God's work, for reasons obviously still veiled in obscurity at this point, since our eyes have not yet become accustomed to picking out the details of this kind of story.

Jesus leads them into a discussion of "the things" that have occurred recently, managing to get Cleopas to say to him, of all people, that he must be the only stranger who does not know what has happened in these last few days in Jerusalem. What is the point here? If nothing else, Cleopas demonstrates that the knowledge of the death and crucifixion of Jesus is very much public knowledge. More than this: in verses 22–24 he reports the astonishing turn of events by which they have all come to see that the tomb is empty, the body is gone, and now the only sure thing is that *nobody really knows what is going on*. Cleopas does not use these exact words, or at least Luke polishes them up if he did, but the point is established as clearly as we could wish. It turns out to be an important point, not just for this story, but for our thinking about interpretation. The facts are all in, as it were, and they do not add up. The tomb is empty; the angels have been seen (by women, which may be why Cleopas is particularly unsure what to make of it, since women's testimony on its own was a much-debated issue at the time); there were all these hopes riding on Jesus; and now nobody knows what to make of it. It is good to read slowly enough to pick up all these details. Sometimes we read biblical stories so fast, and with a kind of vague familiarity, that we can miss the way that the story develops and aims to surprise us.

What happens next? Jesus responds to Cleopas, explaining that on the contrary, all is not lost, but that "it was necessary that the Messiah should suffer these things and then enter into his glory" (v.26). He then interprets Moses and all the prophets for them, they walk on to the village, he stays and breaks bread with them, and in verse 31 their eyes are opened, and at last they recognize him. He vanishes, but they, inspired and now fully energized, return to the apostles and proclaim that "the Lord has risen indeed!" Now it all makes sense. Now they have not just the facts, but a picture that puts the facts in context and adds up. It adds up, let us note, in ways they had not anticipated. Luke first showed us a scene of information with confusion: the necessary prelude to understanding and insight. By the end of the story, the two who set out on the road from Jerusalem are back where they started, but their world has changed. The journey along the road to Emmaus, as captured in this story, invites us to a similar sort of journey in our own understanding: a pilgrimage into insight and wisdom. It is worth picking out in more detail some of the ways in which Luke 24 leads us into our own journey of biblical interpretation.

In his commentary on Luke's gospel, Joel Green suggests the following structure for the Emmaus story:

The Journey from Jerusalem (verses 14–15)
    Appearance, "Obstructed Eyes," Lack of Recognition (16)
        Interaction (17–18)
            Summary of "the Things" (19–21)
                Empty Tomb and Vision (22–23a)
                Jesus Is Alive (23b)
                Empty Tomb, but No Vision (24)
            Interpretation of "the things" (25–27)
        Interaction (28–30)
    "Opened Eyes," Recognition, and Disappearance (31–32)
The Journey to Jerusalem (33–35)[1]

Figure 1. Luke 24 as a Chiasm

It is set out in this way to highlight the "there and back" structure of the story. It starts and ends in Jerusalem, it includes eyes being obstructed and opened, it includes two "interactions" or dialogues on the road, and "the things" which happened in Jerusalem are both summarized and interpreted. At the centre of the story, on this view, is the declaration that Jesus is alive (v.23). This kind of structure of a biblical story is known as a *chiasm*, so-called after the shape of the Greek letter χ (*chi*), which looks like our "X." It is a way of showing that a story has a symmetric structure in itself.

Why would we notice this? It is important to realize at this point that the layout of the original Greek copy of the Gospel of Luke, as of any New Testament manuscript, would be one continuous written text: one letter after another with no breaks between words or sentences or

1. Green, *Gospel of Luke*, 842. His section on the Emmaus story is 840–51.

paragraphs. In fact it was also written in capitals. We can get an idea of the overall effect by imagining reading a Bible that was printed like this:

NOWONTHATSAMEDAYTWOOFTHEMWEREGOINGTOAVILLAGE . . .

There were also no such conventions as bold or italic or underlining for emphasis or subtitles or section headings. (One reason that is given for *why* they wrote this way is that writing materials were expensive and scribes needed to take as little space as possible in copying out texts.) The obvious feature of this way of writing that strikes us, then, is how a New Testament author could particularly emphasize a point. How could they make sure a reader noted that here was a major turning point, or a key moment in the story? We might use a subtitle, or a larger font, or put it in bold text. One equivalent in the first century was to build literary structures into the text.

For instance, you could write with a certain rhythm, so that as one read along they would notice that the author was highlighting something. A non-biblical example of this is the way that Shakespeare's plays often have rhyming couplets at the end of a scene, almost as a coded way of pointing out that the scene is about to change. Or you could repeat a key point twice in similar words: a device known as parallelism. This is very common in, for example, the Old Testament book of Proverbs. When you read, "My child, be attentive to my wisdom; incline your ear to my understanding" (Prov 5:1), both halves of the verse are saying the same thing, as a way of emphasizing the point being made.

The *chiasm* was a slightly more complex structure along the same lines: a short section of text that hinged or pivoted around a central moment, and that paired off elements of the story before and after that central moment. The key point of the chiasm was often to show just what a difference the central moment made. Of course there is a certain creative act of judgment in seeing a chiasm in the text: not all interpreters of the New Testament will agree on whether it is "really" there, but perhaps this is not as significant as one might think at first. A more modest claim would simply be that such an observation could be a helpful way of looking at a text even if it is not necessarily the "right" way of describing that text.

In this particular case, Green's suggested chiasm for Luke 24 seems to fit well enough, and it pivots around the central affirmation that Jesus is alive. In other words: the claim that Jesus is alive (and note that it is presented in verse 23 as a report to be considered rather than as an emphatic conclusion) is the key to seeing how the passage pulls together all that it is saying. To be precise: that Jesus is alive is the key difference between summarizing "these things" and *interpreting* them.

Before we come on to the word "interpreted" in verse 27, there are some other things that we can say about Luke 24, which draw us into the theological significance of the story. We might note that in verse 19 the traveling companions describe Jesus as "a prophet mighty in deed and word." Luke is fond of this way of describing Jesus. Acts 1:1, which refers back explicitly to the Gospel of Luke, calls to mind that gospel by saying that it was about "all that Jesus did and taught from the beginning" (although the translation is debatable, it does not affect this point). The combination of saying and doing, which are really two ways of performing acts of any kind, occurs also in the important story in Luke 4 where Jesus preaches in the synagogue at Nazareth— the real start of his public ministry according to Luke. There his "gracious words" cause amazement, while at the same time he expects his listeners to challenge him to perform the "deeds" which he had previously done elsewhere.

What then is the significance of Jesus being described as a "prophet mighty in deed and in word"? In Acts 7:22 Luke reports Stephen, in his speech to the Jewish council in Jerusalem, describing Moses as "powerful in his words and deeds." Elsewhere, in Acts 3:22, Peter thinks back to Moses and remembers the words of Deuteronomy 18:18 where a prophet like Moses is promised. To understand this we need to grasp something of the unique stature and significance of Moses in the Old Testament.

The so-called five books of Moses, from Genesis to Deuteronomy, were known as the Torah, and formed the foundational document for Israel's faith. This was the basis around which all of the rest of "the scriptures," i.e., the Jewish scriptures, were built. All the scriptures would have been taken seriously as a word from God, but still the Torah always played the foundational role.

We may rightly interpret the Hebrew word *torah* today as "law," and indeed many do speak of "the law" as shorthand for these five books. However, we must recognize that *torah* is so much more than what we tend to mean by "law." Arguably the best translation for the word *torah* is "instruction"—suggesting texts that seek to form a certain way of living. But more significantly, the Torah served as the foundation for all of life and faith for the people of God. Through the Torah, the "voice of Moses" would still speak to the attentive Jewish reader at the time of Jesus. What Christians call the "history books" in the Old Testament (Joshua, Judges, and so forth) were generally known as "the prophets," and thus when Jesus began with "Moses and all the prophets" in Luke 24:27, we should understand this as indicating that he was interpreting all of scripture, in whatever precise state it stood at that time.

In describing Jesus as a prophet mighty in deed and word, Luke is also expecting his readers to pick up an echo of Moses. Here is the one who is fulfilling the role of the long-expected prophet of Deuteronomy 18. Luke is not simply saying, "Jesus is that new Moses." Rather he has in mind the kinds of ways in which first-century believers would have been accustomed to think of Moses: as an authoritative figure, a prophetic figure, a mediator of the presence of God to the people, and so forth. And then in describing Jesus as an authoritative figure, a prophet, and a mediator of God's presence, Luke is inviting his readers to see that Jesus fits as a "new Moses" figure, which would have been understood to be a claim about Jesus' unique position and role in God's work.

This kind of "old *and* new" approach is quite typical of biblical thinking. The point is that the writer takes a familiar way of looking at something well known, and uses it to describe something less well known. "You all know about Moses and how we understand him in such and such a way," the argument might run, "'well, now I am going to describe Jesus in the same way." The writer avoids saying "Jesus is Moses," or to use a similar example, "Jesus is Elijah,"[2] but the conclusion is supposed to be obvious, if you have eyes to see it. Similarly here in Luke 24. Luke leaves us to draw our own conclusion: Jesus is the one greater than Moses who was prophesied, and was eagerly expected. He is a "new Moses" figure.

This kind of theological significance, seeing in Luke 24:19 the drawing of lines of connection between Jesus and Moses, is part of the sensitivity to reading the story which we should be trying to develop as we work with its texture and structure and begin to see what we are supposed to be looking for. It will elude us for as long as we see the goal of biblical interpretation as the extraction of the one right meaning from the text. Biblical interpretation is more subtle than that: it is tied up with the long, slow skill of learning to think theologically.

2. Compare Matthew 11:14 and John 1:21, which relate to the hopes raised by Malachi 4:5.

All of which leads us on to a final point from the Emmaus story, and in its way one of the most important observations about biblical interpretation that we can make. It involves Luke 24:27, a verse which reads: "Then beginning with Moses and all the prophets, he *interpreted* to them the things about himself in all the scriptures." (The emphasis, of course, is added). This word "interpreted" is a version of the normal Greek word for "interpreted." It appears here as *diermēneusen*. If we ignore the *di-* prefix, which loosely suggests some element of interpreting in or through something, we will find that the verb used here is a form of *hermēneuō*, to interpret or to explain. This is the word that gives us the modern English word "hermeneutics"—the art of interpretation, or of explanation and understanding. This is not a technical word that Luke is using, but is simply the normal word for what he wants to say: Jesus *interpreted* the scriptures. Although this particular word does not occur often in the New Testament, this does not mean that the rest of the New Testament is unconcerned with interpretation.[3]

"Hermeneutics" has become a fashionable word for what used to be called simply "biblical interpretation." In fact, the way it is often used, there seems to be no difference between it and "interpretation," and I have some sympathy with those who feel that it is itself a piece of jargon designed to obscure what should be very straightforward: the reading and understanding of the Bible. One sometimes hears it suggested that the church seemed to manage perfectly well without hermeneutics until a few years ago, so why now is there the need for so much to be written and said about "biblical hermeneutics"?

Several things could be said at this point. As noted in the introduction, "hermeneutics" is actually not just interpretation, but it is the evaluation of interpretation too: the whole question of what it means to understand and explain a text, and what criteria there are for evaluating it. But more to the point, the "straightforward" meaning of the biblical text is often a way of saying "straightforward to me," and it does not appear equally straightforward for everyone. In fact, this is precisely one of the issues in Luke 24. All the disciples could read the scriptures and see

3. The word turns up a handful of times in 1 Corinthians 12–14 relating to interpreting speaking in tongues, and also in Acts 9:36 with its other main sense of "translate" to describe a Greek "interpretation" (or translation) of an Aramaic name. There are a few other examples similar to this last one. A different word is used for "interpretation" in 2 Peter 1:20—discussed in chapter 6 below.

what they said, but the "interpretation" which Jesus was about to offer was not one with which they would have been familiar. It is helpful to realize that when we are talking about hermeneutics in connection with the Bible, we are standing in a line of tradition which goes back to Jesus himself on the Emmaus road, conducting a Bible study which it would have been a great privilege to attend, even if Luke did not consider it appropriate to offer a summary of it at this point.

Notice what is happening here. Recall that in the story as we have studied it, there was a general agreement on the "facts"—that, for example, the tomb was empty. It was the interpretation of those facts that was causing the trouble. What made the difference? Not new and better facts that underlined the first set of facts. Facts were not hard currency, such that if you had enough of them they added up to an interpretation. Indeed, they still do not work that way. What actually made the difference was having Jesus give them a way of looking at the Old Testament scriptures which showed them that what had taken place in Jerusalem was after all what should have been anticipated. It should have been what faithful believers were hoping and waiting for rather than a dramatic reversal which called into question all the various hopes around at that time: hopes for a Messiah, for vindication, for God to prove that, somehow, God's side was the right side to be on.

The two travelers on the road to Emmaus recognize Jesus when he eats with them. The way Luke tells the story is clearly designed to call to mind Jesus' instruction to remember him in bread and wine—the meal in Luke 24:30 (and v.35) is presented as a Communion meal. Their eyes now opened to the biblical text; finally the scales fall away and they see who Jesus is. But note that it was only in walking and talking with Jesus that they first had their eyes opened to the biblical text. Their understanding of Jesus gave them access to an understanding of scripture. Their understanding of scripture enabled them to understand Jesus. It was not one or the other, nor even necessarily first one and then the other also, but rather the two together, each feeding into and supporting the other. Thus:

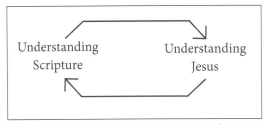

Figure 2. Understanding Jesus and Understanding Scripture

Thus we have a kind of "circle" of understanding, often described as a "hermeneutical circle." In the words of Joel Green, "What has happened with Jesus can be understood only in the light of the Scriptures, yet the Scriptures themselves can be understood only in the light of what has happened with Jesus. These two are mutually informing."[4] But the word "circle," perhaps because of the connotation with the idea of a "vicious circle," tends to give the impression that our interpretation is consigned to go around in circles never getting anywhere, and so this idea is more usually called a "hermeneutical spiral." Each time we go around the circle we get more out of it.

Our reading of scripture deepens as our relationship with Jesus deepens. Our relationship with Jesus becomes more subtle, more profound, as our ability to see him as the fulfillment of all of scripture increases. In this sense, we never arrive at the point where we have finished reading the Bible. Obviously, we can start at the beginning of Genesis and read right through to the end of Revelation, and reach a kind of an end. But every time we come to a familiar passage later in time, we come to it as a different person, changed in who we are, and thus changed in our reading of the passage. This in turn then challenges and changes our relationship with who Jesus is. And so we proceed around and up the "spiral."

The fact of the empty tomb required a framework before it could begin to make sense: the framework provided by the dawning realization that Jesus was alive, and that this was all according to the scriptures. Likewise, the bare text before us, as we read the Bible, also needs a framework before it can begin to make sense to us. Many will be familiar with the experience of patiently reading a Bible passage, or hearing one read out in church, and at the end of it having little clue as to what has

4. Green, *Gospel of Luke*, 844.

actually been said. The words go in, and we may even know the broad outline of what it is about, but the sense of the passage eludes us. When this happens, what we need is a framework—something other than yet more words to explain the first set of words, but some kind of vantage point, or perspective, or "a-ha!" insight which makes us see that *these* words are pointing to *this way* of looking at things.

What then makes the difference between a surface-level reading of the Bible, where we see (or hear) word after word without really comprehending the sense of the text, and an act of interpreting the Bible with understanding? In Luke 24, the difference centers on Jesus. One can read the New Testament for many reasons, but for Christians concerned about the nature of God and what sort of life God would ask us to live, we read the New Testament not just as words on a page, but as Christian scripture. Indeed, some have said that to read the Bible "as scripture" is already to offer an interpretive framework, and a theological one at that.[5] It is to say that God is involved in the interpretive task. To read the New Testament as Christian scripture is to see Jesus in the light of the scriptures, and the scriptures in the light of Jesus. It is to bring scripture reading into the heart of what it means to be spiritual, and vice versa.

There are a lot of ways that this point needs to be clarified and handled carefully. For one thing, the idea that Jesus stands at the centre of the Christian practice of reading scripture needs to be brought into dialogue with the traditional Christian theological claim that God is a Trinity of Father, Son, and Holy Spirit at one at the same time. This is not the place to discuss the Trinity, but only to offer a brief suggestion as to how that dialogue might go. Where Luke 24 takes us as far as "Christocentric" (Christ-centered) Bible reading, this need not stop us, on other grounds, developing a fully Trinitarian Bible reading to *develop* this perspective, and not to undermine it. This is particularly true when it comes to articulating a Christian reading of the Old Testament, as we shall consider in a later chapter. We would also need to reconsider, if what has been said so far is true, just what we meant in the first place by "facts," which is one reason why I occasionally retain "scare quotes" around the word, to indicate that a fact is not always a fact, depending on who is looking at what, and who is trying to say what.[6] All of this is

---

5. The phrase "as scripture" was given prominence by the title of Childs' book: *Introduction to the Old Testament as Scripture.*

6. The notion of a "fact" is something of a modern one anyway. Alasdair MacIntyre

the concern of those interested in "theological hermeneutics," a some-what forbidding label for the study of the important issue of how to read the Bible theologically.

For us it is enough to note that the simple attempt to read the Emmaus story in Luke 24 led us straight to theological questions as it introduced us to the task of reading the Bible in its theological context. Without these questions, we might well return from the seven mile walk to Emmaus every bit as confused and disheartened as we began it, only now we would be worn out into the bargain. Suitably inquisitive, however, we are drawn in—eyes opened—to see that all the scriptures point to Jesus, and that our growth as Christians depends on both our experience of Jesus *and* our engagement with scripture, not just one or the other. Far from being worn out by the walk, we would only wish that the seven miles had been longer, and that we might have been able to overhear more of what Jesus said on the journey, as we began to grasp what it meant to read the Bible in its theological context.[7]

offers the wonderful epigram: "facts, like telescopes and wigs for gentlemen, were a seventeenth-century invention" (MacIntyre, *Whose Justice*, 357).

7. Luke 24 has been something of a focal point for thinking about how we should read scripture. For further reflections see Hauerwas, *Unleashing the Scripture*, 47–62 (a sermon on Luke 24 entitled "The Insufficiency of Scripture: Why Discipleship Is Required"), Moberly, *Bible, Theology, and Faith*, 45–70, on "Christ as the Key to Scripture: the Journey to Emmaus," and Wright, *Challenge of Jesus*, 114–33, on "Walking to Emmaus in a Postmodern World."

2

A Historical Book

The Pharisee and the Tax Collector

LUKE 18:9–14

You believe that:

- the scriptures are the word of God
- they apply to all of life
- it is important to interpret them properly
- God still speaks through those scriptures today
- God's word is for everyone, even those who do not realize it

Who are you?

YOU ARE SOMEONE WHO takes scripture very seriously. Maybe you would be happy using the adjective "evangelical" to describe yourself, or maybe not. But as you read down the list you find yourself strongly agreeing with all these statements. They capture something important about your own outlook on the Bible. You might even go further, and argue that these are the precise points at which today's Christians need to stand firm against the tide of woolly-minded loose thinking which so undermines the church at the present time. Well, you may be glad to know, you are not alone.

You may not be so glad to realize who your fellow defenders of the faith are, agreeing with all those points as they read down the list.

They are the Pharisees, those well-known heroes of the New Testament. Can that be right? This sets us off on the historical trail that we shall be exploring in this chapter.

The story of the Pharisee and the tax collector (or better: toll collector) is a short parable told by Jesus "to some who trusted in themselves that they were righteous," in the words of Luke 18:9. The basics of the story are simple, and well known in that "well known" sort of way that tends to obscure what is actually going on. Two men go up to the temple to pray. The Pharisee congratulates himself on all the good things he does, while a toll collector simply asks for God to be merciful to him, since he is a sinner. The second one, and not the first, goes home "justified."[1]

Who are we as we read this story? Clearly we would not wish to be the Pharisee, who slots neatly into our "bad guy'" role. We are the "sinner," not perhaps a toll collector as such, but at least someone who knows the right answer: that we are righteous by the grace of God and not because we have impressed God in the first place. The moral is obvious: Pharisees get what is coming to them. Do not be like them. Confess your sin instead, and God will welcome you in.

There is, of course, a profound half-truth in this, which is what ensures this interpretation endures and is so easily the one that can be preached from this passage. The truth is that the confession that "I am a sinner" is precisely what qualifies me to receive this "righteousness" which God offers, even if at this point we have done no work in deciding what such a concept as "righteousness" could really be. The problem is rather with the other half of the interpretation, which suggests that we are not supposed to be like Pharisees, who are often seen as the archetypal religious hypocrites. It is here that we need to begin to do some serious historical homework.

For many Bible readers today the Pharisees have a walk-on part, existing solely to provide sermon illustrations for Jesus. They are seen to typify all that is wrong with the religious establishment, of which we are proud (in a humble sort of way) not to be a part. A moment's reflection should indicate that the whole picture is bound to be a lot more

---

1. Reading this passage in English obscures the link in Greek between "righteous" in verse 9 (*dikaios*) and the word "justified" in verse 14 (from *dikaioō*, to justify). English effectively lacks a verbal form "to righteous" (or "be righteoused")—the nearest would be "to make/be made right."

complex than this. Who were the Pharisees? Who did *they* think they were, for instance? What would they have said were their aims and driving ambitions? What did the word "Pharisee" mean anyway? In a flash of inspiration we might consider turning back to the Old Testament to see something of their background and origin, and there we meet with a puzzle. In the Old Testament the Pharisees are conspicuous by their absence. So where did they come from? Who are these people?

The word "Pharisee" appears to derive from the Hebrew word meaning "to separate."[2] Thus a Pharisee is a separated person, but separated from what? To answer this we need to know something of the so-called "intertestamental period," that time between the Old Testament story and the arrival of Jesus. It is a little hard to determine when exactly the Old Testament story finishes, since several Old Testament texts (notably prophecies) are very hard to date, but the main outline of the story seems to end with the restoration of Jerusalem under Ezra and Nehemiah in the fifth and fourth centuries BC.[3] The broad plot outline of the Old Testament takes us from Egypt through the exodus, into the promised land, through the turbulent centuries of Israel's self-governance under Saul, David, and Solomon, the split of the kingdom into two, and the eventual exile of both halves, with the Southern Kingdom finally falling to the Babylonians in about 587 BC. The return to Jerusalem authorized by the Persian king Cyrus is led by Ezra, and the city of Jerusalem largely restored under Nehemiah. And there the story more or less fades out, with the obvious question being: What happened next? Do things just carry on in largely mundane ways until the dawn of the New Testament? Was it, in a sense, happy ever after once Ezra and Nehemiah had done their work?

No it was not. The trials and difficulties, as well as the successes and victories, of the intertestamental period rival anything in the David and Solomon era, but since they are not in either half of the Bible they are much less well known. I choose my words carefully here, because the place where some of these stories can be found is in the apocrypha, a collection of books occasionally included in some Bibles, and then ap-

2. The origins of the Pharisees are somewhat difficult to pinpoint. The word "Pharisee" starts to be used in the late 2nd century BC.

3. The book of Daniel is an exception, as we shall see below. A particular kind of account of later times is offered in Daniel 11, but it takes a good prior knowledge of events of the third and second centuries BC to follow it, so most Bible readers, in my experience, are none the wiser.

propriately printed between the two halves, or testaments. In particular the book of 1 Maccabees tells the story of the Maccabean family resisting the then-ruling Seleucid dynasty, and restoring the temple sacrifices after the temple had been the subject of attack by Seleucid ruler Antiochus Epiphanes IV in 167 BC.[4]

This whole period of intense persecution from 167 to 164 BC is the occasion for the later, somewhat mysterious chapters of the book of Daniel with all their talk of the "abomination that causes desolation" (Daniel 11:31; 12:11) occurring on the temple site. One possible reason why Daniel is written in the unfamiliar style of "apocalyptic" may be that it is written at just such a time of persecution and threat to the people of God (a theme we will revisit when we consider the book of Revelation later). One of the fundamental claims of the Maccabean revolt, of the desire to reclaim for God what had become compromised and defiled, was that a new obedience to God was required which would not tolerate any form of compromise. Here we need to see especially that the typically modern dissection of life into separate compartments such as spiritual, religious, social, political, personal, and so forth would not have made any sense at this time. Life was a whole, and if one belonged to God, then every aspect of one's life must be dedicated to God.

It is broadly against this background that the Pharisees developed. They were dedicated to the written Torah, but by this time the written Torah continually had to be reinterpreted for new situations for which it had not originally been intended. This ongoing work of interpretation had given rise to a body of oral tradition that would subsequently grow into the massive collection of rabbinic writings that we possess today. To put the point in its simplest form: the Pharisees represented an attempt to adapt traditional faith to a new situation, and to avoid what they saw as the mistakes of earlier generations who had made peace with ruling empires only to see their own worship and integrity compromised by those in power.

When we rejoin the story of God's people in the New Testament, we find that Israel was now under Roman rule, through a system of local rulers called tetrarchs. The word "tetrarch" originally meant "ruler

---

4. The account of the rededication of the temple is in 1 Maccabees 4:36–61. The festival which remembers this, and which continues to this day, is *Hanukah*, or the "feast of dedication," which is the feast occurring in John 10:22, another New Testament reference which cannot be understood from the Old Testament alone.

of a fourth part," but it came to refer to the various delegated rulers of Israel and the surrounding area, such as Philip in Luke 3:1. Israel found itself in a complex world of political and social relationships where the Pharisees stood in basic opposition to those among the Jewish people who sought co-operation with Rome as the way forward. All of this, we might note, is immediately relevant to reading the New Testament in today's equally complex social and political world, where Christians differ so widely in their attitudes to the appropriate relationship between the church and the wider state and society.

To many in Israel at the time, the Pharisees were threatening because they appeared to stand for all that was "religiously correct," and yet they did it in unnerving and complicated ways which were bound up with their ongoing interpretation of Torah. Perhaps, after all, they were right, and perhaps too many people simply dealt with the conflicts between the Torah and society by ignoring or spiritualizing away the awkward details of Moses' words. If you were among the crowds listening to the parables in Luke 18, you were probably thinking that it would of course be wonderful to be as dedicated to God as the Pharisees were, but you do not have the time for it, since dealing with all the requirements of daily life leaves you exhausted enough as it is.

What are we to make of this? The first point to make is that our historical homework immediately paints a rather more sympathetic picture of the Pharisees than the New Testament does. Secondly, if we have begun to understand why the Pharisees thought the way they did, then we may notice something familiar about a key issue which they faced: everything they did was to be motivated by a deep love for God, but all too easily they could cross over a fine line and end up thinking that they were alright (or all righteous?) with God *because* they were doing all these things. At this point they could lose sight of the gracious basis on which God had invited his people into the covenant in the first place.

The question persists, then, as to why Jesus is so forthright: "Beware of the yeast of the Pharisees, that is, their hypocrisy" (Luke 12:1). In one of the most damning passages of the entire New Testament, Matthew has Jesus saying, "Woe to you, scribes and Pharisees, hypocrites! For you tithe mint, dill, and cumin, and have neglected the weightier matters of the law: justice and mercy and faith" (Matthew 23:23). The Pharisees according to Jesus are hypocritical, although we should note that he is not saying that it was a mistake to tithe herbs, only that other matters were neglected which were "weightier"—that is, which had more significant consequences.

To hold these observations together with our more sympathetic picture of the Pharisees requires us to know a little more about the Jewish world that lies behind the gospels. It is not too much of a simplification to pick out four separate groups of the time, and then observe that the vast majority of Jewish people were not members of any of them. Most were "the people of the land" (the *am-ha-aretz*) whose daily lives revolved around work and subsistence, with only the Sabbath set aside as a day when the work could stop. Of these four groups, the Pharisees are the ones we read most about in the New Testament.

The Sadducees, about whom relatively little is known, are mentioned in a handful of biblical texts, notably the passage where they construct the unlikely scenario about one bride for seven brothers who all die one after the other.[5] They are not interested in the pastoral impact of this on the poor woman, but on the technical issues this raises concerning who would be married to whom in the life to come. Their point was that such a case seems to make a nonsense of the whole idea of the resurrection life. Indeed the Sadducees are mainly known today for what they did not believe rather than what they did: "The Sadducees say that there is no resurrection, or angel, or spirit; but the Pharisees acknowledge all three" (Acts 23:8). This is one important clue to the reason why the Pharisees turn up so often in the New Testament, at least in contrast to the Sadducees.

We should briefly mention the other two types of people. First there were the "Essenes," noted for their separatist existence out in the hills surrounding Israel. Little was known about them until the discovery of the so-called Dead Sea Scrolls in a cave at Qumran, along the western edge of the Dead Sea, between 1947 and 1956. There are, in all likelihood, no examples of Essenes in the New Testament—not even John the Baptist. The description of the Baptist in the gospels, and in particular his apparent desert existence, had seemed to some to make him a prime candidate for this identification, but in the end the evidence is inconclusive. Secondly there were the "Zealots," of whom Simon is explicitly identified as one in Luke 6:15, and perhaps the "bandits" on

5. It occurs, with some differences, in all the first three gospels: Matthew 22:23–33// Mark 12:18–27//Luke 20:27–40.

the cross are also examples.[6] There was a well-known Zealot uprising in AD 6, which is mentioned in Acts 5:36–37, albeit somewhat problematically since Luke's account of who was involved (or at least his report of Gamaliel's account of who was involved) does not fit well with what we know from elsewhere. Nevertheless, even taking a generous view of how often the Zealots are mentioned in the New Testament, they do not have a particularly high profile.

None of these other groups really demand much attention in the New Testament, so why the Pharisees? We are now in a position to answer. It is because they were so close to grasping what it was all about. Their concern for God and for the proper response to God's word was fundamentally what God would have wanted. Their passionate desire to do what was right was in itself wonderful, but in their concern for demarcating precisely what was right and wrong they betrayed something more important: an ability to focus on what was truly central to the life of faith and obedience. One might almost say that Jesus was so hard on the Pharisees because in their effort to clarify the right way to God they were in fact blocking the doorway to the kingdom of heaven, and nobody else could get past. They had their faces pressed up against the glass, and nobody else could see in.[7] Jesus would have been delighted to welcome them in, and indeed he eats with them and generally mixes with them in the gospels, but they in turn drive others away with their relentless attention to the detailed interpretation of the minutiae of the Torah and its oral traditions.

We do not need to rely solely on this kind of broad-brushstroke reconstruction of what must have been the problem, because we actually have considerable documentation of some of the Jewish interpretations of the law during that period. The oral traditions surrounding the Torah are written down for us in a collection from around the end of the second century AD entitled the *Mishnah*,[8] while an enormous sprawling rabbinic commentary on it, known as the *Talmud*, occupies many

6. This too is inconclusive. The word used in Matthew 27:38, 44//Mark 15:27 to describe the two "bandits" crucified with Jesus is *lēstēs*, which is the same word used when Jesus calls the temple a den of "robbers" (Matthew 21:13//Mark 11:17//Luke 19:46).

7. This is not quite how Jesus puts it in his startling verbal assault on them in Matthew 23, but it is close; see verse 13 especially.

8. For a convenient edition see *The Mishnah: A New Translation*. Translated by Jacob Neusner. New Haven, CT, and London: Yale University Press, 1988. This is the translation of the *Mishnah* quoted in this chapter.

large volumes. Now it is true that these sources themselves need careful historical handling, and that they tend to represent only certain lines of thought in first-century Judaism—mainly the more liberal tendencies which survived into the second century when these books were written down—but even so we may see some general insights into what sorts of issues were at stake in the time of the gospels. For our purposes, we need not worry unduly about exactly how much the concerns of the *Mishnah* were the same as the concerns of the Pharisees in Jesus' day.

The most celebrated saying in the *Mishnah* is this:

> Moses received Torah at Sinai and handed it on to Joshua, Joshua
> to elders, and elders to prophets.
> And prophets handed it on to the men of the great assembly.
> They said three things:
>   "Be prudent in judgment.
>   Raise up many disciples.
>   Make a fence for the Torah."
> (Tractate *Abot* ("Fathers") 1:1)

Here we find the chain of tradition stretching back to Moses, the ongoing work of wise discernment entrusted to that tradition, and in the final command, the idea of "making a fence for the Torah." What does this mean? It basically requires the erection of a "safety zone" around the actual requirements of the Torah, so that even if one transgresses the safety zone, the commands of the Torah themselves are not breached.

For example, one must not work on the Sabbath. This much is more than clear in the Torah: in addition to the well-known commandment from the Ten Commandments, there are such straightforward passages as Exodus 31:12–17. In Numbers 15:32 the Israelites find a man gathering sticks on the Sabbath. After some confusion it is concluded that this breaks Sabbath too. Since transporting objects from one place to another is work, the idea becomes that one must not carry things around on the Sabbath. But then, what if a beggar approaches your house with a begging bowl and thrusts it into your hand. Can you hand it back to him, even if it means transporting an object on the Sabbath? Well, it depends on who initiates the movement, or on whether a greater act of generosity is being performed in feeding the beggar, and in various circumstances one person or the other, or both, are exempt from violating the Sabbath. Confused? Tractate *Shabbat* 1:1 will sort it out for you in a variety of cases, relating variously to both the one inside a property and the one outside the property. The fact that this single issue in itself ends up comprising fifteen subpoints indicates the inevitable complexity of this line of thinking. If you do in fact manage to tithe all your herbs correctly then one thing is certain: you will be busy. Arguably so busy that you will never get round to weightier matters.

But all of this is an exercise in hedge-building, and the real problem comes when you spot your neighbor not exactly breaking the Torah, but breaking the hedge around the Torah, and you fail to spot this crucial difference. The law certainly did not require fasting anything like as often as twice a week: once a year was all that the Torah required, although it is clear that the practice had become somewhat more common than that by the time of the Pharisees.[9] But fasting more regularly was not a requirement of the Torah, whatever its merits. What now will the Pharisee in Luke 18 say if his neighbor fasts only as often as the Torah itself requires?

And what now will we say? Perhaps we too take God's word seriously, and are concerned to construct our own hedges around it lest we might transgress God's commands. We may be concerned to know whether what we are doing is right in God's eyes, whether it be going to church every Sunday, giving to charity, driving always within the speed limit, generously leaving a tip at the end of a meal in a restaurant, or rightly paying airport tax to fly out of our own international airport but then refusing to pay "bribes" in far-flung cafés and airports, to take a select list which might have gone down well with our Pharisee in Luke 18, if he were to find himself mysteriously transported to the departure terminal at LAX. Meanwhile, he is still standing and praying in the middle of the temple for all who will hear him, and in this, we should note, he is not so unusual. This is not necessarily a strange kind of pride in being spiritual. Rather it is the kind of prayer we find in the *Talmud*, where the rabbis taught that a man might pray, as he leaves worship, "I give thanks to Thee, O Lord my God, that . . . Thou hast not set my portion with those who sit in (street) corners, for I rise early and they rise early, but I rise early for words of Torah and they rise early for frivolous

---

9. Fasting is not all that prominent in the Old Testament. The only expectation in the Torah is once a year, on the day of atonement (Leviticus 16:29, 31). People also fasted for a range of reasons including as part of mourning, or in penitence. In later times we find indications of four annual fasts being observed (Zechariah 8:18–19). Expectations about fasting are clearly also an issue in some gospel stories (e.g., Mark 2:18–28).

talk . . . I run to the life of the future world and they run to the pit of destruction."[10] Our Pharisee may simply be giving thanks for the very things we would think it appropriate to give thanks for.

We may read Luke 18:9–14, six short verses which see the Pharisees get their just desserts, and we may think that this is the way it is supposed to be: the self-righteous brought down low and the lowly lifted up. This last part is true, but we have nevertheless read Luke 18 from the wrong position, since now the parable has simply confirmed what we already thought:

> The parable is usually "understood" as a reassuring moral tale which condemns the kind of Pharisaism that everyone already wishes to avoid. A parable which originally had the function of unsettling the hearer and overturning his values now serves to confirm him in the values which he already has.[11]

If we have learned to read the parable in its historical context, it should indeed unsettle us greatly.

Commentators have tried very hard to worry away at verse 14, where the toll collector went home "justified", and have sometimes said that here we surely do not have the full-blown Christian doctrine of justification, with all the staggering implications this would have for, of all people, a toll collector. Toll collectors were as near to the bottom of the pile as made no difference: they made their living charging extra on the Roman tolls which were in place at just about every border crossing in the area, and thus they not only annoyed everyone who tried to travel anywhere, but they served as a constant reminder of the much-loathed Roman governance which lay at the root of so much of Israel's trouble in the first place.

If such people are now going to get justified, and Torah-abiding religious leaders, the upright pillars of society, are going to be thrown out into the cold, then something is happening which will do more than just annoy those who are doing alright by this present system. This is the kind of offensive and subversive teaching that could get you into trouble. On reflection, it does seem unlikely that at the root of the persecution Jesus faced, persecution even to death, was the basic moral point: "Don't be like one of those hypocrite bad guys, but look out for the poor good

10. From the *Talmud: b. Ber.* 28b.
11. Thiselton, *Two Horizons*, 14.

guys." That is a message that Hollywood, for instance, would have little trouble portraying. But a gospel message—the one that comes into focus when we read the Bible in its historical context—is an altogether different proposition. Anyone taking the Bible seriously as a word from God, and attempting to interpret it faithfully for today's world, needs to think twice before responding to Luke 18:9–14 by praying, "God, I thank you that I am not like the Pharisee."

What have we learned as we return from the detailed world of historical reconstruction? If we learn to see the Pharisees—and many other historical components of the New Testament world—in the right focus, and with the right associations, then we allow the biblical text to speak in something like the voice it intended.[12]

We may want to defend our own approach to scripture on the grounds that it is God's word, and therefore needs to be interpreted to cover every eventuality. We may start to suppose that this requires copious lists of rules and regulations about what is and is not permitted. We may even do all of this thinking that it is no more than simple obedience to the task of taking the Bible seriously. But once we have done our homework we realize that, for all its obvious merits and good intentions, this is to stand in the shoes (or sandals) of the Pharisee. Conversely, we may have all kinds of good reasons for distrusting today's equivalents of the toll collectors, who perhaps make money out of running a big lottery, or over-charging on simple car repairs because the insurance will pay, or working for newspapers which enjoy lampooning Christianity as a ridiculous and hypocritical bunch of people trying to impose moral standards on people. But when such people ask the God of mercy to have mercy, and acknowledge their sin and ask for it to be washed away, then God will indeed wash it away, and send them home justified. Every time we think we are nearer the first of these two stereotypes, then we should watch out, for we are likely to be brought down low. Every time we recognize ourselves in the second, we should rejoice, because we are encouraged to believe that we shall go home righteous.

---

12. For those now wishing to explore further, let me recommend Theissen, *Shadow of the Galilean*, a novel written by a New Testament scholar(!) which draws on a lot of interesting background material to depict the world in which the gospel stories take place.

3

A Literary Work

Luke's "Orderly Account"

WHATEVER ELSE IT IS, the gospel of Luke is a story; a narrative.[1] How should we read a story? Most people know that a good way to read a story is to start at the beginning, go on until the end, and then stop. Most people who read the Bible probably know this too, but in practice they rarely, if ever, do it. There are at least two reasons for this. First, most of us do not read two-thousand-year-old stories most of the time, and thus the amount of background detail we do not grasp is unusually high when we read a story like Luke's gospel. In theory, though, this is no different from reading *Pride and Prejudice* and needing to know about social conventions in early-nineteenth-Century England. Many readers seem to get by (although, of course, others do give up). Secondly, most of the stories we read do not come to us as part of an authoritative book. While the nature of biblical authority is always hard to define precisely, as we shall see in a later chapter, it must have something to do with making an impact on the way we live. But how? What does it mean for a story to have an impact upon us? Here is where a biblical story really needs to be handled as a story.

---

1. I shall not enter into any discussion of what makes a "story," and whether it is or is not the same as a "narrative." I do not intend these terms in any theoretical sense, and shall use them more or less interchangeably.

31

Anything plucked out of its story setting (or its "narrative context," as scholars like to say) may set off quite inappropriate lines of thinking. Here is Luke 10:4: "Carry no purse, no bag, no sandals; and greet no one on the road." The first part of this need not suggest to us that purses or wallets are "unbiblical," any more than the second part is a basis for ignoring people you walk past as you are out and about. Equally, when we arrive at Luke 22:36—"now the one who has a purse must take it"—this is not a "contradiction" of the previous passage. Neither should the startling conclusion to this verse—"the one who has no sword must sell his cloak and buy one"—draw the unwary into investing heavily in shares in sword manufacturing companies.

Just as the previous chapter started with a short passage from Luke and then took a lengthy historical detour in order to come back and read it afresh, so this chapter will begin with what looks like a particularly uninteresting verse tucked away in the middle of the gospel, and then try to build up a narrative framework around it to give us new ways of looking at Luke. The focus here is on the literary features of the text: reading the Bible as a literary work and with awareness of what kinds of questions this raises for us.

We should note right at the outset that Luke himself raises literary questions for us. In the preface to his two-volume work (Luke–Acts), he gives us his explanation for what he has written, namely "an orderly account of the events that have been fulfilled among us" (Luke 1:1 and also 1:3). Luke's work is not the breathless note-taking of Mark's gospel, which rushes from story to story with barely a pause for breath. It is the considered work of an editor (or "redactor," as editors are usually known in biblical studies) who has read all the sources and is here compiling an "orderly account." But which "order"? How does Luke put his account in order?

We can start to respond to this by comparing the gospels of Matthew, Mark and Luke.[2] When we cross-compare them we soon notice that the order of the events within the three gospels varies considerably. Luke's order does not therefore necessarily correspond closely to the historical order of events as they took place, or if it does then Matthew and Mark do not. In other words, Luke has other reasons than historical reportage

---

2. These three are commonly called the "Synoptic Gospels," with "synoptic" here meaning "seen together," and thus all covering basically the same material, or all "seeing" the same thing.

for putting his account in the order he does, and that is what we shall pursue here. A literary approach to Luke's gospel wants to know what *Luke* meant to say by telling his story *this* way, in contrast to approaches which might be focused instead on what Jesus meant, or what happened and when. This focus on Luke, rather than on the Jesus that Luke writes about, throws the emphasis on the writer, who is also a "redactor," as we just noted. The approach therefore includes within it questions that fall under the heading of both "literary criticism" and also "redaction criticism," a technical name for interpretations that ask about the work of the "redactor'" (or editor). My own view is that these two approaches overlap somewhat, and that combining them leaves us asking good literary questions that are all part of how we generally think about stories. On the whole we shall avoid talking about "redaction" wherever possible.[3]

The verse we shall begin with is a brief description of Jesus in Luke 9:51, which the NRSV translates, accurately, as "When the days drew near for him to be taken up, he set his face to go to Jerusalem." This may not seem like much to go on, but let us see where it leads.

Luke 9:51 is a "getting underway" verse. It is like that part of the story that says "they loaded up the car and set off." Maybe it is of no significance at all, except that Luke several times stops and makes this kind of observation. Consider how he reports Jesus' words in chapter 13: "I am casting out demons and performing cures today and tomorrow, and on the third day I must finish my work. . . . I must be on my way, because it is impossible for a prophet to be killed outside of Jerusalem" (13:32–33). In 17:11 we read, "On the way to Jerusalem Jesus was going through the region between Samaria and Galilee." At first sight, if we consult a map at this point, this does not seem the quickest route to take, except that direct travel through Samaria would have been quite exceptional at the time, with Samaritans being so severely disliked by the Jewish population at large. Even though the "parable of the good Samaritan" is fresh in our memories at this point in the gospel, perhaps Luke is simply acknowledging that Jesus took the standard Samaritan-avoiding route. Nevertheless, there is something interesting going on here, since back in 9:52 Jesus *was* going through Samaria. It is hard to avoid the conclusion

---

3. I simplify, of course. Redaction criticism is particularly well suited to looking at how Luke may have edited his source material, especially if that source material was Mark. This important line of enquiry, however, lies outside of our concerns here.

that if Jesus were simply engaged in transit to Jerusalem there would have been quicker ways of getting there.

In Luke 18:31, Jesus takes his disciples aside and says, "See, we are going up to Jerusalem," and four verses later they are on their way, passing Jericho as they go. All these references to movement and purpose have led scholars to propose the name "Luke's travel narrative" for this central section of the gospel.

Once we start to think in terms of a "travel narrative," we begin to notice all kinds of markers of movement. Indeed, to pick up the hints we had in chapter 1 on the Emmaus story, the "journey" theme is one of the ways Luke tells his overall story, and for good reason. We note that in 10:1, a verse that is obviously mainly about the sending out of the seventy, Luke adds, "every town and place *where he himself intended to go.*" In 10:38 they are going merrily on their way. In 13:22 Jesus goes through "one town and village after another." This whole theme is magnified in chapter 19, which begins in Jericho, noted in verse 11 as being "near Jerusalem." Whether one notes that Jericho is near Jerusalem or not tells us more about the one doing the noting than about the geographical locations involved: it is noted here because Jerusalem is looming into view in the (middle) distance. In verse 28 Jesus goes on up to Jerusalem, and soon he is drawing near to the city and then entering the temple. Time after time Luke points out Jesus' progress. Why?

One of the ways in which an author can highlight a major point in the narrative is by playing with the speed of the story. On a very simple level this can be seen in Martin Kähler's delightful characterization of Mark's gospel especially, but of all the gospels, as "passion narratives with extended introductions,"[4] one of those great oversimplifications that captures a more important big picture than all the many details it omits. Since about half of Mark's gospel is taken up with the passion narrative, clearly one of the great emphases of Mark is the story of the death of Jesus. The time spent in telling that part of the story is proportionately far greater than the time spent telling the rest of the (preceding) story. Likewise, Luke moves briskly through the stories of Jesus' birth and childhood, and slows the pace down when he arrives at the synagogue in Nazareth so that we are enabled to hear the words of Jesus as he preaches from Isaiah. The most obvious of these "slowing down" moments occurs here in chapter 19 as we finally arrive at Jerusalem, the city that has been

4. Kähler, *Historical Jesus*, 80.

in view ever since 9:51. We shall reconsider shortly just why there is no obvious moment of closure in the story at the point where Jesus does finally arrive there.

It is hard to capture this kind of pacing in a narrative in our world of short hypertext links and sound-bite attention spans. Films compress entire novels into two hours of screen time, but in their own way they have their own devices to tell you how fast time is going. We are familiar with the love story which is established in painstaking detail, before several weeks or months pass in a few moments while music plays over the dialogue as we cut in rapid transition through a representative selection of shots of the happy couple engaged in day-to-day pursuits. They laugh and grin their way through both their relationship and narrative time. Then we pick up the story again as the music fades and we refocus on the next episode to be shown at normal speed. Sometimes we achieve the same effect by having a narrator's voice superimposed on the story: "And it came to pass, in that time, that a great famine came upon the land . . ." The narrator speaks in a kind of omniscient "view from nowhere" voice. In so doing, the author redirects our attention to a new section of the story, and then leaves us to it again.

That is exactly what happens in Luke 9:51. In chapter 9 we have been reading happily along about the story of the transfiguration, that odd moment where Jesus meets with Moses and Elijah up a mountain, and then there is various business concerning demons and exorcism, when suddenly, almost as clearly as the voice from the sky at Jesus' baptism, the voice of the narrator breaks in to make an announcement: "When the days drew near . . ." In fact, the Greek at this point becomes somewhat formal, just the kind of stilted announcer's voice which tells us—without any bold, italic, or underlined font—that a new section of text is beginning. A bumpy, over-literal translation of the verse and the succeeding passage would give us this:

> [51] When drew near (in fulfillment) the days of his assumption and he set his face to go to Jerusalem. [52] And he sent messengers before his face. And, going, they entered into a Samaritan village to make it ready for him [53] but they did not receive him, because his face was going to Jerusalem . . . [56] They went to another village. [57] As they were going, in the way, . . .

Any self-respecting English translation of this passage would rightly smooth a lot of this out, such as the repeated "face," or the constant use of the verb "to go" or "going," and this is only fair for a translation that is setting its sights on the main picture of the story, which we are in the middle of hearing. But in so doing we miss the deliberate slowing effect, the focus, the indication that here something new and important is happening.

What is the key to this strangely translated passage? The setting of one's face to a task is an idiom which still survives in English today: the sense of purpose, resolution in the face of hardship and difficulty, and overall that sense of taking on a mission which is just what characterizes Jesus here. The "going" is so obviously a feature that we should pause to consider just what it can indicate. It seems to highlight the "journey" image noted above. It is worth looking at this in more detail.

In 9:57 Luke has Jesus and the disciples "going along the road." The word "road" (*hodos*) is the same word that simply means "way," as in "they were going along the way." It is no coincidence, then, that in the book of Acts, the title "The Way" becomes a kind of label for the early Christian movement, still unformalized and known by many different names, but six times it is "The Way."[5] Clearly this sense of Christianity as "the way" represents the faith as a forward-moving way of living: life with a purpose, perhaps. It is captured particularly in the famous words of Jesus in John 14:6 ("I am the way . . ." [*hodos*]). One of the things Luke seems to want to communicate is that the Christian life is itself like a journey. It is the following of Christ, not necessarily knowing where that journey will end, or at least not knowing all the places it will take in *en route*. It is a dynamic and ongoing experience as much as (if not more so than) the attainment of a status. To be a Christian is not to arrive already at some new place, but to embark on a new journey.

Luke highlights that journey in 9:57. It is a journey *shown* by the way he tells the story, rather than being explicit in what he says about what happened. In other words, it is what we might call a literary journey, doubtless with a historical backdrop, but where any particular historical journey is not really the focus. With this journey in our sights, we can now revisit the question of where Jesus is going.

Two points will help us here. The first is to note more carefully the word used to initiate the journey description, where we read (back in 9:51 again) that what were drawing near were the days of Jesus' assumption (*analēmpsis*), or "taking up." Which taking up is this? It seems likely

5. In Acts 9:2; 19:9, 23; 22:4; 24:14, 22.

that the "taking up" of Jesus in view here is his ascension, although arguably it could also be a word used to describe his death, raised up on the cross. A reason to prefer the ascension view will become apparent in a moment.

Secondly, if Luke 9:51–56 is setting out the beginnings of a journey of major importance, then perhaps we should be looking for clues around this section of Luke as to where Jesus is said to be going. We know that Jerusalem is in view, but does Luke say anything else about this journey? If we now turn to the surrounding stories we will notice something about the way Luke tells the transfiguration story in chapter 9.

The transfiguration story is unusual, even by the standards of the gospels. Jesus meets with God on a mountain. In fact he meets with Moses and Elijah, with all the symbols of divine presence in place too (the dazzling white; the changed appearance, the glory, the voice from the cloud, and so forth). The whole scene is reminiscent of Moses' various meetings with God up a mountain (the stories of Exodus 24 and 34). It is not that anybody quite believed that God was high up in the sky and thus that a mountain was a good way to get to him, but rather that here was a place set apart from the day-to-day cares of the world; a place where one could make space for meeting with and receiving from God. Perhaps Moses and Elijah symbolize the law and the prophets, although probably it is at least as significant that they both, in different ways, were thought to have cheated death: Moses with an unknown burial place (Deut 34:6), such that he was still present and still "spoke" wherever the Torah was taken seriously, and Elijah with his whirlwind and his chariots of fire (2 Kings 2:11), as if riding into a sunset whose details we shall pick up shortly.

The transfiguration story (Luke 9:28–36) occurs also in Matthew 17:1–9 and Mark 9:2–10, but with a significant difference. The basic outline is the same, but the version in Luke contains an additional central section of the transfiguration story, in 9:31–32.[6] In particular the first of those two verses tells us what Jesus was talking about with Moses and Elijah.[7] The verse tells us that they were speaking about Jesus' "de-

6. Just to note: this is exactly the kind of observation that earns the label "redaction criticism," as we discussed above.

7. Of course we do not actually know what the three of them said, since presumably no one, not even Peter, overheard it. Luke's account comes through some chain of interpretation—perhaps from Jesus and/or Peter— and thus the precise words Luke uses are Luke's and not necessarily Jesus' or Peter's. In fact this simply underlines that

parture, which he was about to accomplish at Jerusalem." The word for "departure" here is *exodos*. It can mean "death," which is kept in view here by the non-specific word "departure." One cannot complain that the translation is wrong, but one thing that is lost is the resonance that this word would have had for the people of God, the resonance with the "exodus" itself from the book of that name.[8] Israel's very identity was forged in and through that exodus, as they were delivered from slavery to Pharaoh to slavery to God.[9]

What does Jesus envisage as he contemplates the future of his ministry, standing on the mount of transfiguration? He is already embroiled in the life of an Israel of conflicting messianic hopes, with religious authorities who are worried that his relaxed approach to some points of Torah-interpretation is just the kind of thing causing Israel trouble. Perhaps he is trying to think through the shape of his calling in the light of all this? Maybe Jesus is looking at a traumatic ministry every bit as decisive as a new kind of exodus: a new leading of the way out of the old world and through trials to come (not a trial by sea, but certainly trials of some sort), and then followed by the glorious arrival in a "new land" as yet unimagined.

Could this new exodus involve a "taking up"? Here we recall the word used in Luke 9:51 (*analēmpsis*), which we next encounter in Acts 1:2, where Luke casts a backwards glance into his gospel to see Jesus being taken up to heaven. If we had but time and knowledge of the Greek translation of the Old Testament,[10] we would find this same word used in 2 Kings 2:9 as Elijah turns to Elisha, his soon-to-be promoted assistant, and asks what he can do for him "before I am taken from you." Finally, we recall that Elijah's extraordinary departure—between earth, sky and, in some strange way, death—saw him ride a whirlwind into heaven on a chariot and horses of fire: *taken up* into whatever it is that awaits us beyond this life.

---

we are engaged here in the literary analysis of how Luke has told his story, rather than in historical reconstruction.

8. The English word "exodus" derives from the Latin *exodus*, which itself comes from the Greek *exodos*—"exit." The second book of the Old Testament has the English name it does because of its Latin/Greek title. In Hebrew it was known by the rather less illuminating "these are the names," its opening words.

9. This way of putting it can be seen in verses such as Leviticus 25:55.

10. Known as the "Septuagint," abbreviated to LXX. We shall look at this a little more in a later chapter.

Now we begin to see why Luke 19 was so reticent about trumpeting the moment of arrival. When Jesus arrives in Jerusalem it is a goal of sorts, but it is not in fact his final destination. Jerusalem was to be the place where Jesus, having set his face to his mission, to the way ahead, would be *taken up* in order to fulfill that mission. The real goal of the journey lies beyond: in heaven. Luke 9:51 gives us an image of Jesus setting his face to return to heaven, by way of Jerusalem. It is perhaps not too much to claim that Luke 9:51 is the pivot—the turning point—of the overall story of Luke's entire gospel.

This observation fits too with an interesting feature of the genealogy of Jesus in Luke. It is only in Matthew and Luke that we find genealogies of Jesus, tracing his line back through the generations to their different starting points. In Matthew chapter 1, that most extraordinary choice for a first chapter for the New Testament, the line goes back to Abraham, the father of the faith (Matt 1:2). This tells us, if we have literarily-attuned eyes to see it, that a major concern of Matthew's whole book is going to be Jesus' role in relationship to the traditions and practices of the people of God down through the centuries.[11] In Luke chapter 3, the line goes back further, to God (Luke 3:38). It is presented in a very unself-conscious way, simply continuing the line back through Seth, then Adam, and then God, as if Luke were really only saying what everyone knows. But why God, and why only here? Is it because Luke wants to say that Jesus comes from God, or from heaven: the abode of God; the place where God is. In Luke's telling of the story, Jesus begins by coming from heaven, down to dwell among us through the nativity story—shepherds, embodied humanity and all—and begins his ministry, right up to the point where he sets his face to be taken up. This new purpose is to go to Jerusalem, yes, but to go beyond Jerusalem and return to the Father, to heaven. Luke's entire gospel, perhaps, is one big *chiasm*—one big "there and back" structure—and it turns around the central moment of 9:51.[12]

The other gospels have similar "turning point" moments. In John 12:23 "the hour has come," and there is a very similar sense of moving from an account of Jesus' ministry among humanity to the pursuit of his glorious return to heaven. In Matthew and Mark, the turning point

---

11. What in later times could be called the issue of the relationship between Judaism and Christianity.

12. For an elegant reading of Luke's gospel in this way see Gooding, *According to Luke*, 9 and throughout.

seems to gravitate more naturally around an incident recorded also in Luke 9:18–20, the debate about Jesus' identity where Peter answers that Jesus is "the Messiah of God."[13] The effect is largely the same: a new sense of purpose and direction which turns Jesus' ministry towards its goal. Luke may have read Matthew and Mark, of course, and got the idea from them, or at least if they were already available then they may be among the accounts he says he has considered in Luke 1:1. Either way, this shows that all of the gospels, and not just Luke, have particular ways of telling their stories, and that at least sometimes we need to think of how a verse or saying or incident works in the wider context of the overall gospel story if we are not to miss some important aspect of it.

An opposite way of putting the point is equally important. If we realize that some verses are basically doing the job of building up the bigger narrative, drawing out the bigger picture, then we will be freed from trying to find some kind of self-contained theological message in every detail of the biblical text. Some parts of it will be helping us on our way, putting us in touch with the wider journey that the text is inviting us to take, and enabling us to grasp that bigger picture. These texts will not make great sermon texts in themselves, but without them, more obvious sermon texts would lose their context, and in the end would lose some of the power which comes from seeing them in context.

In these first three chapters we have only scratched at the surface of Luke's "orderly account." The insights from the various passages we have considered invite us to read with opened eyes to see what is really going on in these sometimes too familiar texts. As I have tried to show through these three chapters, it is the biblical text itself which invites us to take up these different hermeneutical approaches. Our eyes may be opened by theological, historical, and/or literary concerns. There are many other angles of approach we could consider, but these three categories give us a helpful initial framework for thinking about the different types of approach available.

If I have a reservation about how we have proceeded thus far, it is this: what we have said about interpreting the Bible has perhaps made it sound like there is one kind of thing which is "the biblical text" in front of us, and that we have been learning a few ways of reading which might work for any biblical text. Certainly we can profit with any text by asking theological, historical, and literary questions of it. However,

13. Mark 8.27–31 (recounted also in Matthew 16.13–20 as well as Luke).

in my judgment, there is one big stumbling block to this kind of general hermeneutical approach to "biblical texts." The stumbling block is that there is a fundamental structure built into the Christian Bible which separates all its texts into two different categories: the Old Testament and the New Testament. This affects many of the ways in which we should read biblical texts wisely, or to put it another way, part of that wisdom consists in knowing when and how to do things differently with the Old and New Testaments. The next chapter explores this basic two-testament structure of the Bible (which we shall also return to in Part Two of the present book). The chapter following then attempts to show that we can still make good use of our theological/historical/literary framework when reading Old Testament texts, even if the details of how it works out may be different.

4

Two Testaments

Why Read the Old Testament?

Some years ago I was interviewed for a job to teach the Old Testament in a theological college. On the train on the way to the interview I was mugging up on the latest and greatest insights of Old Testament studies, trying to sound fluent in all manner of hermeneutical models, and master the ability casually to toss key names into my various answers, in order to impress those who would interview me. First, however, I met a student panel whose opening question, delivered with unself-conscious directness, was, "Why should we bother with the Old Testament, then?" The question comes back to mind whenever I lead a church study day on a subject like "Reading the Old Testament." Indeed it has broadened out into reflecting on the very common opinion heard in our churches that since we have Jesus and the New Testament, why do we need to trouble ourselves over this difficult and problematic ancient book with its God who seems to be so angry? This chapter offers some ways of beginning to answer these questions. If we can get our thinking straight on *why* we read the Old Testament, then that will leave us better placed to think about *how* we should read it. Oh yes: my answer to that question in the interview was "I don't know." This was true, and I still got the job, but if asked today, I might try to answer it like this.

There are many different answers to the question: why read the Old Testament? It is a kind of hermeneutical question, about biblical texts, though it is not directly a question about hermeneutics. To some extent, the answers one might find convincing will depend on factors of background and tradition, but only to some extent. Some proposed answers are simply inadequate to the nature of the Old Testament. I shall suggest that there is no one single answer, and that wisdom lies in holding together several different possible reasons for persevering with the Old Testament. Furthermore, different reasons are more significant for different parts of it.

Here is my prototype attempt to sketch out the basic argument in diagrammatic form:

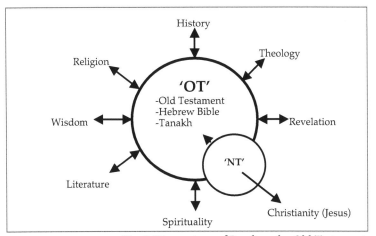

Fig. 3 Dimensions of Reading the Old Testament

Three points need to be discussed with regard to this diagram. First, it shows the Old Testament as the object of attention. As we shall discuss later on, the name "Old Testament" is a value-laden label, and not a neutral description. We may for the moment simply point out that "why read the Hebrew Bible?" is a different question from ours, though obviously with many points of overlap.

Secondly, the arrows in the diagram are all double-headed because our interest can run both ways. For example, what does the Old Testament tell us about history, as well as how does the Old Testament match up to our understanding of history? This is a question about the specific agenda being brought to bear in any given case.

Thirdly, these "dimensions" are a representative list, and other headings could be equally appropriate. Nevertheless, the headings chosen are an attempt to cover certain key angles of approach, and many of the alternatives could perhaps be grouped within or alongside these cat-

egories, or perhaps in some distribution of them. Thus one thinks of specific interpretive agendas (feminism, for example), or church traditions
(such as Methodism), or alternative ways of conceptualizing key areas
of inquiry (ethics, perhaps, alongside "theology" as such). The chosen
headings are all at least familiar possibilities in terms of the profile of
the Old Testament in the church and the academy, and will demonstrate
enough of a range of options to substantiate the point being argued. If
the analysis could be extended to other categories, then so much the
better. We turn to a brief discussion of these different dimensions.

1. HISTORY

We can read the Old Testament because we are interested in what happened. We will not have to read very far (Leviticus, perhaps) before we
realize that answering the question "what happened?" is no more the
guiding principle behind the Old Testament than it is the New, although
along the way we will learn a great amount about a lot of ancient history. Some Old Testament texts are very concerned to situate themselves
historically (e.g., 1–2 Kings, Haggai). Others are almost impossible to
date, or at least have no apparent interest in being dated (e.g., Job, Joel).

The Christian canon labels some of these books as "historical
books," while the Jewish canon opts for "former prophets" as well as
several "writings." It may be best simply to say that all the Old Testament
books fall somewhere along a spectrum that runs from being focused on
history to not being focused on history. The relationship between these
books and the modern discipline of "history" is of course a problematic one. The extent to which historical writing can or does ever portray
"what happened" is a matter of considerable debate these days, and the
discussion over the historical status of the Old Testament "version" of
history is currently a major focus of academic attention. There is not a
great deal of archaeological evidence concerning large stretches of the
Old Testament, and when inscriptions and artifacts do turn up, unsur-
prisingly, people find ways of fitting them into incompatible interpretive
schemes. This happened in 1993–94 with the first inscriptional evidence
concerning David (or was it?), the *bytdwd* or "house of David" inscription from Tel Dan.[1] Nevertheless, you *can* walk through Hezekiah's tun-

1. For a not uncontroversial analysis see Athas, *Tel Dan Inscription*, and his update
article, "Setting the Record Straight."

nel (mentioned in 2 Kings 20:20) and you *can't* find any archaeological evidence of Ai being where it was supposed to be in Joshua 8 (in fact, more precisely, you can find Ai, but it's not there when Joshua 8 takes place). There is a clear difference between these two types of evaluation which is worth holding on to no matter how flexible we may wish to be regarding "history."

To venture a massive generalization: "biblical archaeology" was a big subject in the mid-twentieth century, and it aimed to correlate the Old Testament with archaeological evidence. There has been some success. But overall interest has moved on, and now people are often more focused on questions of historiography (the nature of history writing), and socio-political agenda (e.g., who wrote this and what were they trying to prove?). In short, we can of course read the Old Testament because our interest is historical, but this should not be our only, or even our main, interest, and the results will often be inconclusive.

2. THEOLOGY

Moving around the circle: we can read the Old Testament because we are interested in theology. We can seek theological understanding in the narrow sense of "a knowledge of God,"[2] or in the general sense of understanding life in terms of God's being and God's action in the world. A lot of the Old Testament is evidently good material for this task: Psalms which reflect on why God does or does not act; visionary prophecies seeking justice and/or righteousness; bracing judgments on political events traceable to the abandonment of worshipping the God of Israel ... "Why do the nations conspire and the peoples plot in vain?" (Ps 2:1). "God (the Lord) is merciful and gracious, slow to anger, abounding in steadfast-love" (Exod 34:6). "Your prophets have seen for you false and deceptive visions" (Lam 2:14). And so forth.

That we can do theology in dialogue with the Old Testament is not in doubt. Precisely what that theology is, of course, is a matter of endless dispute among those engaged in the task. Open the average book on Old Testament theology and you will most likely find epic discussions of how to go about doing it. Some organize all the material around a central concept, such as covenant. Some look for the heart of Israel's proclamation passed down from generation to generation. More re-

---

2. Noting that the word "theology" comes from the two Greek words *theos* and *logos*.

cently there has been an acknowledgement that the many voices of the Old Testament do not all obviously say the same thing all the time. One can find studies these days entitled *Theologies of the Old Testament*: it all depends on where you are looking from in the social and economic spectra of the various stages of life in ancient Israel. A massive and influential study by Walter Brueggemann cuts to the finished Old Testament but still speaks of argument and counter-argument: *Testimony, Dispute, Advocacy*, as the subtitle of his *Theology of the Old Testament* has it.[3] This is a wonderfully stimulating area to explore, complicated still further if we broaden the horizon to the question of a Christian "biblical theology." Here one can argue that the "center" of the Old Testament, if it has one, lies outside it (e.g., in Jesus, or in a full-grown Christian theology).

This is not the place to evaluate all these ways of approaching the theology of the Old Testament. Suffice it to say here that they all represent ways of engaging with the Old Testament that take its theological dimensions seriously.

3. REVELATION

We can read the Old Testament because it is revelatory. This angle is clearly close to the previous one, with the theological perspectives perhaps arising out of some of our other concerns than just the reading of the text. Some passages of the Old Testament clearly focus on the revelation of God: Exodus 3 and 6, Isaiah 6 in some ways, in fact—significantly?—many of the most well-known passages. In other texts God is revealed in the course of the action. But the point of saying that the Old Testament is revelation is usually simply that it stands as part of the Christian Bible, and therefore the "why read it?" question hardly arises. This view would say that we read it because it is inspired, part of Holy Scripture, and (depending on how one cashes out that claim exactly) it is true, authoritative, or in some way essential for the Christian. All these terms will be explored further in a later chapter. For now there are a few simple points to be made which relate specifically to the Old Testament focus of this discussion.

First, if this is our answer to "why read the Old Testament?" then it is unlikely to be a complete one, or rather: it will not explain how it is that

---

3. Brueggemann, *Theology of the Old Testament*. His subsequent work, *Old Testament Theology*, is perhaps the best straightforward introduction to this area at present.

this revelatory/inspired book ends up saying such problematic things as Deut 7:2; Ps 137:9 or Ezra 10:11, to take only three of the most perplexing examples. It is far from simply self-evident to claim that the Old Testament always pulls through with good Christian theological insights.

Secondly, and for similar reasons, it is problematic to make the familiar argument that if the Old Testament is revelation then it is simply true, which would settle the "why read it?" question. The main problem with this is that it uses the hammer of "truth" as if it were the only tool in our interpretive toolkit. What makes a psalm true? Is "The one who lives alone is self-indulgent" (Prov 18:1) true? Are laws or commands true? What makes a story true? The Hebrew word for truth, *'emet*, can perhaps be understood as "faithfulness": this might give us a sense of the Old Testament being true as meaning that it is entirely trustworthy, or reliable. This is a better kind of claim, but still not a straightforward one to defend. Which of Isaiah 2:1–4 or Joel 3:9–10 is the reliable word today, for example?

Most importantly, the Old Testament–New Testament structure to the Bible is I think more significant than this straightforward "it's all revelatory" argument allows. This brings us to the next angle of approach.

4. THE NEW TESTAMENT: A CHRISTIAN READING?

We can read the Old Testament as preparation for, or as an integral first part of, the Christian story of the whole Bible. This argument sees the Old Testament as playing a key role in our understanding of Christian faith. After all, Jesus himself read it as his scripture.

Note that this acknowledges that there is a significant (theological) difference between the Old Testament and the New Testament. In the New Testament, as we learn at Sunday School, the answer is always Jesus. In the Old Testament this is not the case, at least not in anything like the same way, but to understand Jesus we do need to know something about the Old Testament. Why does he quote Psalm 22 on the cross? Why do the gospel writers use Psalm 118 as they describe his entry into Jerusalem? What is the significance of "Isaiah 53 language" in the passion accounts? The *New* Testament, as its name suggests, was never intended to be read as a separate book in its own right: it was always a supplement or continuation (or climax?) to something else.

One of the most debated areas in hermeneutics today is the question of what is "theological" about this approach to the biblical text. Is it (rightly) acknowledging the theological nature of the texts themselves? Is it a concern brought to the Old Testament by the reader if that reader happens to be a Christian? If we do not read the Old Testament back through the lens of the New Testament then are we really reading the *Old* Testament at all?

These discussions sometimes take place on an "all or nothing" basis: either everything stands or falls on reading the Old Testament as Christian scripture, or the interpretive bottom line is that the reader should bracket out their own personal faith when they interpret texts. My aim in suggesting these different dimensions of the reading of the Old Testament is to argue that there is a place for Christian reading of the Old Testament: it offers one compelling reason to read it without being the only reason. We also need to acknowledge that reading the Old Testament simply to "defend" or "support" Christianity frequently results in superimposing a particular Christian message on some texts not intended for that purpose. Sometimes the Christian dimension of the text emerges from taking it on its own terms anyway.

5. SPIRITUALITY

We can read the Old Testament for spiritual illumination. My guess is that this is the default position for many Christians (and arguably, though in a different way, for Jewish people reading their own scriptures). It is probably seriously underrepresented in academic books and journals. The sad result of this is that "spiritual" insight is left to less careful or well-founded works, operating on a popular level, often with no reference to what we know about ancient Israel and its traditions. In extreme forms, this argument might even suggest that there is no fundamental difference between the reading of the Old Testament and the reading of the New Testament: it is all simply "Bible reading" and we are to come to the text for a word from the Lord, whatever text we read. On that account, we could take Joshua 1:9 ("Be strong and courageous; do not be frightened or dismayed, for the Lord your God is with you wherever you go") as an inspiring promise for our own situation, as simply as we can take Galatians 2:20 (which I choose more or less at random) as a word for today.

While many Christians obviously do find great encouragement in taking scriptural verses this way, there is usually some deeper kind of interpretive method (or "hermeneutic") at work here which makes sure that we pick the right kind of verse to make this approach work. The danger is that we screen out all those parts of the Old Testament which do not give us this kind of instant encouragement: we can simply make it reflect back to us what we want to find in it. It is debatable whether we need to go to all the trouble of reading the Old Testament anyway if all we want in the end are a few words of encouragement.

A real engagement with the Old Testament and spirituality will instead ask after the ways in which the text describes or imagines the disciplines of life with God in ancient times. It will assume that these practices cannot be translated to today without due attention to historical and cultural factors, but it will (generally) assume that with sufficient care the translation not only can, but should, take place. To take one example: Old Testament thinking about the routine of Sabbath rest has become prominent in theological and spiritual reflection. This has little to do with legislating what you can or cannot do on a Sunday, in contrast to some of the ways we saw that the Sabbath was handled in earlier centuries, but equally it has little time for thinking that every day without end should be treated exactly the same. The re-emergence of annual Christian festivals, conferences, and events could also be considered in frameworks drawn from the Old Testament.[4]

6. LITERATURE

We can read the Old Testament because it is great literature. This is a view that can be shared by people of all faiths or of none, and as such it has a widespread apologetic value in university departments. Perhaps, for this reason, it is a bit overplayed. It is not obvious that there are vast hordes of people wanting to plough through Samuel and Kings because they tell a great story, even though, as has often been pointed out, the story of Saul is a tragedy *par excellence*;[5] and for my part I would love to see someone like Peter Jackson make a film version of the David story

---

4. On the general point see the probing work of Sheriffs, *Friendship of the Lord*, who addresses the rhythms and rest issue also (291–363).

5. See for example Exum, *Tragedy and Biblical Narrative*, 16–42, beginning with an overview of many previous studies on the theme.

with the same epic scope and vision as the Aragorn storyline from *Lord of the Rings*, and perhaps then the numbers of people wanting to read the book might increase. . . . But "the Bible as literature" is still the Bible being read and considered, and these days C. S. Lewis' famous complaint that it can represent "reading it [the Bible] without attending to the main thing it is about" seems unduly pessimistic.[6]

Interestingly, a focus on the narrative quality of the Old Testament text has become a major feature of Jewish approaches to scripture, often pursuing detailed studies of the poetic and literary qualities of the (Hebrew) text. These are, without doubt, eye-opening to those raised on considering the Old Testament as a doctrinally-bound contribution to Christian theology. The widespread popularity of *The Literary Guide to the Bible* is at least evidence of the appeal of these approaches.[7] In the extreme version of this, Jack Miles' *God: A Biography* reads the Old Testament as a single narrative biography of God.[8] It is very interesting—why does God stop talking, for example, after his final speeches in Job?—but it does leave the question: how should we evaluate the interpretive framework with which this undoubtedly operates?

7. WISDOM

We can read the Old Testament for its insights into wisdom. Wisdom is back on the agenda of theologians at present. David Ford writes of churches today: "I see the most important item on their theological agenda at present being the education of their general membership for living in truth and wisdom."[9] And where else should we look for biblical wisdom if not in the so-called "wisdom books" of the Old Testament?

Traditionally (or at least over the last hundred years or so) wisdom was marginalized in Old Testament studies because it did not seem to relate obviously to what were supposed to be the key themes of the Bible: salvation, redemption, perhaps creation. There were various and often understandable contextual factors for this, notably the desire of some German theologians in the 1930s to avoid thinking that truth about God

---

6. Lewis, *Reflections on the Psalms*, 3. As his fuller discussion makes clear, Lewis knew that it was more complex than this.

7. Alter and Kermode, *Literary Guide*.

8. Miles, *God*.

9. Ford, *Long Rumour of Wisdom*, 14. See more extensively his *Christian Wisdom*.

could be deduced from the natural world, as a safeguard against certain forms of natural theology. But we should accept that the Old Testament itself does have a large interest in practical questions of wise living, and in that this interest is shared quite widely in the ancient Near East, it does indeed raise questions about the overlap between the faith of Israel and other faiths. If we are interested in wisdom, that comes with the territory: history testifies amply that Christians, for example, do not have a monopoly on it.

In fact, the present book is based in large measure on my own conviction that wise reading is absolutely key in our consideration of scripture. My own view is that many parts of the Old Testament, not just the "wisdom literature," are relevant for this task. Wisdom may not be the only issue, but it is a major one.

8. RELIGION

We can read the Old Testament because of what it tells us about Israelite (and indeed other) religion, and perhaps by implication, religious practice today. If we define religion as what happens when people engage in the worship of a deity, and try to live accordingly, then evidently there is plenty of material for this. Books on *The Religion of Ancient Israel* abound, many of them designed as introductory Old Testament textbooks. Such an approach masks many problems, not the least of which is the relatively modern development of the category "religion," which is not always well suited to capturing the dynamics of the Old Testament text.[10] The surface-level problem is simply that the material for constructing a history of Israelite religion is distributed across disputed and ever-changing archaeological reconstructions, and in a collection of literature that does not present its material in a way that allows the task to be done easily. Reconstructions of Israelite history today often depart massively from the picture presented in the biblical texts.[11]

I suspect that none of these problems should stop us from attempting to understand what happened in temple worship, or who funded history writing, or the social location of prophecy, to take standard examples; but they do perhaps help us to see that "religion" is a rough

10. This is a problem with much of our Religious Studies terminology, even including words like "monotheism."

11. See Soggin, *Israel in the Biblical Period*, 1–28, for a standard, brief, and helpfully simplified account.

and incomplete answer to the question "why read the Old Testament?"'
Religious concerns, we might also note, tend sometimes to satisfy themselves with observing diversity in Old Testament texts without asking
the further (harder) question of why such diverse texts were ever held
together in the canon in Israel. Did Israel see things differently at different times? Did Israel's understanding *improve* over the centuries (and
how would we tell?); and if so, is it of vital importance that we date all
the books correctly so that we can know which understandings are the
"right" ones? Simple answers to these questions are, inevitably, also simplistic ones.

Thus we are led back to questions of history and historical method,
at the beginning of our circle, as well as to the vexed area of relating
Israel's life and faith to that of the Christian church (which were some of
our other categories above). We come full circle.

All the above angles of approach contribute something to answering our question. Arguably they all contribute to saying why it is the
whole of the Old Testament that should be read, even as we acknowledge
we read it one part at a time. This is worth saying because it is the experience of reading this or that selected portion of Old Testament text
which usually provokes people to their greatest frustration with the Old
Testament, whether on a moral, ethical, spiritual, or theological level.
Individual verses or passages from the ancient world do not, it seems to
me, stand much chance of flourishing if taken out of their wider canonical context, and dropped down into our late-modern capitalist society.
It is the canonical picture as a whole that offers an alternative vision
of life to the one pushed at us relentlessly in Western culture today. I
suppose that if I had to give a short answer to the "why read the Old
Testament?" question then that would be it: the canonical vision of the
whole Old Testament offers us something which stands over against our
own culture(s) and draws us in to engagement with the God of Israel,
who is also the God made known in Jesus Christ. Perhaps too often this
is not well understood without the backing of something like the longer
multidimensional sketch offered here, which is why on the whole I would
suggest that there is not really a satisfactory short answer at all.

The other factor introduced here is how to assess whether we have
understood this "canonical vision" properly, or rightly, or correctly, or
whichever evaluative word we may wish to use. This moves us from "why
read the Old Testament?" to "how should we read the Old Testament?"

Clearly the two questions are not unrelated, but my suspicion is that we might do well to benefit from reflecting more carefully on the former in order to help us with the lengthy, complex, and demanding tasks of the latter. The next chapter will take us through some Old Testament texts, drawn from the book of Isaiah, in order to revisit our suggestions about historical, literary, and theological context and show how they might work in practice with an actual set of Old Testament passages.

5

An Old Testament Example

Reading Isaiah

ISAIAH (CHAPTERS 1, 6, 7, 36–37)

Let's start with a word for the perplexed—you are in good company:

> They [the prophets] have a queer way of talking, like people who, instead of proceeding in an orderly manner, ramble off from one thing to the next, so that you cannot make head or tail of them or see what they are getting at.
>
> ~ Martin Luther[1]

ISAIAH IS THE MOST visionary, and in many ways the most famous, of all the Old Testament prophetic books. The downside is it is also one of the most forbidding. It has earned itself the traditional label of "the fifth gospel" in the history of Christian interpretation, because of the heavy use made of it by the New Testament authors as they talk about Jesus. Yet many readers today feel overwhelmed as they begin to read it, wondering how to make sense of its huge scope and wide-ranging detail. Readers may also feel intimidated by the long-running discussion amongst scholars about how many Isaiahs' there were, and when they wrote, and what sort of difference this makes. For readers of this chapter, the good news is that we will not have to worry about any of that on this

---

1. Quoted in von Rad, *Prophets*, 15.

occasion.[2] Here I hope to encourage you that you can still make good progress by thinking about historical, literary, and theological perspectives with various texts in the book, even without understanding all the wider issues.

With this in mind, experience suggests that it is better to make some progress on chapters 1–39 before worrying about how the whole book fits together. So we will look at a few highlights from these chapters on the principle that we should work towards more complex issues by starting from passages we *can* understand. We shall pay some attention to what sorts of issues are clarified by reading Isaiah as a book of Christian scripture. In particular, we shall consider the question of how some of the more famous prophecies informed New Testament ideas and Christian thinking about "fulfillment." Admittedly, our study of Isaiah would be easier if we did not try to do this, but then it would not really be engaging with the task of reading Isaiah as a book of the Christian Old Testament. There are many other ways to read Isaiah, but this one will keep us busy enough.

The best way to see how different angles of approach affect the kinds of questions one might ask about Isaiah is to take an example. Isaiah 7 is a particularly good example, because it can occupy its reader with historical questions, or literary ones, or theological ones about its role and placement in the overall book, and indeed in the overall Bible. These last questions, the theological ones, we shall call "canonical" questions since they are about the role and status of the passage or book in its canonical context.

READING ISAIAH 7

Verses 1–2 give the historical context, though they are packed with information that is not easy to digest for the average reader. They focus our attention on events surrounding the smaller of the two divided kingdoms, the Southern Kingdom (Judah). A map is also helpful to follow the story: try sketching one out as you follow through the chapter. The nations and people involved are:

---

2. On another occasion, with different passages in the book, it might still be helpful. I have offered a brief overview of the issues in Briggs, *Reading Isaiah*, 14–17.

Nation (in verse 1):	Judah	Aram	Israel
Which is:	the Southern Kingdom	Syria—to the North East	the Northern Kingdom
Capital city:	Jerusalem	Damascus	*various*
Also known as:	House of David		(Tribe of) Ephraim
King:	Ahaz	Rezin	Pekah

If you check the dates of these kings you will find that this is about 735 BC. The reason that Aram and Israel have allied themselves together is given in verse 6: they wish to install their own man as king in Jerusalem. (This set of events is often referred to as the "Syro-Ephraimite War.")

One of the reasons the passage alternates between so many descriptions of who is who and what is where may be for rhetorical effect. Note verses 4–5 for example, the repeated reference to "the son of Remaliah." This is King Pekah, of the Northern Kingdom (cf. verse 1 and also 2 Kings 15:23–25). But perhaps Isaiah wishes to downplay his significance: not even worth naming? Not worthy of respect? The last man standing when Ephraim has been cut down (as verse 9 puts it)—why would anyone be afraid of him? The chart above may be what we need to follow the story along, but it must not replace awareness of how the text is actually scoring points left and right as it goes.

The Lord commissions Isaiah in verse 3, and gives him an oracle to take to King Ahaz in verses 7–9. This includes the striking wordplay, which translates rather nicely into English: "If you do not stand firm in faith, you shall not stand at all" (verse 9),[3] or as N.T. Wright has suggested rather more idiomatically: "trust or bust."[4] In fact, when this Hebrew text was translated into Greek (in the Septuagint version as used by the early church), this line became "if you do not believe, neither shall you understand." As such, it was often cited by Augustine in his famous description of Christian faith as the pursuit of the mysteries of God, captured in the Latin phrase *fides quaerens intellectum*: "faith seeking understanding."

Either way this is a powerful verse, and a powerful assurance to Ahaz: trust in God and trust in his ability to sort out the geo-political

3. Or in Hebrew: *'im lo' ta'aminu / ki lo' te'amenu.*
4. Wright, *Jesus*, 259 n.55.

problems of the day, and hear the ringing promise regarding this threat, that "it shall not stand/it shall not come to pass" (verse 7).

So you are King Ahaz, and you have just met Isaiah out by the upper pool, and heard these great words. What would you do now?

a) Go home and relax?

b) Commit yourself to prayer in hope of a miraculous deliverance?

c) Call up King Tiglath-Pileser and ask the Assyrians for help?

Although the book of Isaiah does not explore this, Ahaz's actions after this oracle are described in 2 Kings 16:5–20, which is worth reading at this point. He contacts the king of Assyria, further to the northeast than Aram, and allies himself with him. This is surely not what Isaiah meant by "standing firm in faith."

Now, in Isaiah 7:11–12, God seems to offer Ahaz a second chance for a word of support or comfort. But armed with this information from 2 Kings, one might suggest that Ahaz's apparent piety in verse 12 is rather more likely a form of stubbornness and a refusal to let God set the agenda. Which brings us to the weary God of verse 13, and the chance to read the famous verse at 7:14 in context: "Therefore the Lord himself will give you a sign. Look, the young woman is with child and shall bear a son, and shall name him Immanuel."

Verbs in Hebrew do not naturally fall into present or past tense; it is the context which suggests to us how to read the tense of the verb. As a result, this verse can be read as either "a young woman is with child" or "a young woman will be with child." Furthermore, when the verse was translated into Greek in the Septuagint, the word for young woman (*'alma*) was rendered by *parthenos*, which means "virgin." Now in the context of the events described in Isaiah 7 the prophecy is fairly straightforwardly that a young woman who either is or will shortly be pregnant will have a son called "Immanuel" (which is Hebrew for "God with us"), and that in the time it takes for this child to grow in the ways described in 7:15–16, the Syro-Ephraimite threat will be over. This is in fact what happened. The Assyrians captured Damascus in 732 BC, and the Northern Kingdom in 722 BC. It is often said that the young woman of verse 14 would have been known to Ahaz, and perhaps the child was his son, Hezekiah (here given a sign-name, Immanuel).

Does this mean, then, that Isaiah 7:14 is fully understood in these historical terms? Not really. If we ask the further question of how Isaiah

7:14 functions in Christian scripture, we need to reckon with the way in which it is quoted about Jesus (and with reference to a "virgin") in Matthew 1:22–23. Matthew finds in Isaiah something he wants to say about Jesus: God's extraordinary provision, met in a child, transforming the world situation, and rightly described as "God with us."[5] The historical prophet Isaiah, meanwhile, was talking to King Ahaz in the middle of a war, where a prophecy concerning 700 years in the future was hardly the right word for the moment. The one oracle has (at least) two different settings and two different types of fulfillment. In our reading of the Old Testament today, it is important to remember that prophecy can be fulfilled in more than one way. In this case we may also argue that the final editor(s) of the book of Isaiah were already aware that there might be multiple levels of fulfillment regarding 7:14. They would know that it would point in the first instance to Hezekiah, but in the light of Hezekiah's own later failings it would have a further (future) figure in view.[6] It is interesting to note that the clearly defined historical context which we encountered at the beginning of the chapter seems to fade from view by the time of the oracles in 7:18–25, as if to suggest that the enduring value of these passages will transcend their original historical setting.

In reading Isaiah 7, what have we been asking? We have asked historical questions about what happened. We have asked some literary questions about how the text communicates its message. We have asked "canonical" questions about how the impact of the text is shaped by its location at this particular point in the two-testament Christian Bible. This is basically our familiar little map of three broad types of question to ask. Sometimes one question or the other comes to the fore, but often a combination of them is useful for understanding the force of the text. Let us now illustrate this claim further with some other examples drawn from the main first section of the book of Isaiah, chapters 1–39.

THE HISTORICAL FOCUS PROVIDED BY 701 BC

After the showdown of Isaiah 7, what happened next? We noted above the fall of the various kingdoms in the late eighth century BC. Assyria,

---

5. The Hebrew is again *Immanuel*, as in Isaiah 8:8, as well as Matthew 1:23, where it is put into Greek and begins with an "E": *Emmanuel*.

6. See the helpful discussion in Seitz, *Isaiah 1–39*, 60–75.

the eighth century "superpower" which caused so much trouble, was increasingly upstaged on the international scene by threats from Egypt in the south and the emergence of Babylon in the east under King Merodach-Baladan. All this predated the founding of the powerful neo-Babylonian dynasty under Nabopolassar (the father of Nebuchadnezzar) in 626 BC. While Babylon would be the major threat of the sixth century, it was one nation among many back at this point. Meanwhile, in 704 BC, King Sennacherib of Assyria came to the throne.

Events of this period come to a head in the story told in Isaiah 36–37. This basically tells a story set in about 701 BC. In broad outline: the Assyrians lay waste to Judah, besiege Jerusalem, and appear to be forcing it into starved submission. Assyrian envoys at the wall—led by the "Rabshakeh"[7]—threaten, insult, and ridicule Hezekiah and his men, in fact with Sennacherib meeting the representatives of Judah at the very place where Ahaz met Isaiah, on the highway to the Fuller's Field.[8] Is this supposed to remind the reader that God has offered prophetic insight once before in such a situation? Once again Isaiah tells them that God is in control. In fact he does this not once, but twice: 37:5–7 and 37:21–35. The story then comes to a startling end in 37:36 with the sudden intervention of the angel of the Lord slaughtering 185,000 Assyrians in the night, never more memorably translated than in the KJV: "and when they arose early in the morning, behold, they were all dead corpses" (37:36). At which point Sennacherib goes home.

Unusually for an Old Testament narrative, we have an alternative account of this whole episode, from Sennacherib's perspective, in his annals. What does he say happened? To paraphrase: he recounts how he extracted a massive payment from the besieged Judahites, ranging over vast numbers of people, horses, gold, silver, and other plunder, after which he simply "departed." End of story.[9]

There are a lot of texts to juggle here, including another different version of the whole saga in 2 Chronicles 32, which we cannot go into

---

7. The NRSV leaves this term untranslated. The word refers to the "chief cup-bearer," a position we might understand as a "communications officer." The NIV offers "field commander."

8. Compare Isaiah 36:2 with Isaiah 7:3.

9. Sennacherib's account is available in most books where ancient Near Eastern texts are gathered together for Old Testament study. The version used here is from *COS*, 2:302–3.

at this point. Just focusing on the main ones we are considering, the comparison of these texts is illuminating:

2 Kings	Isaiah	Sennacherib's Annals
18:13, 17–18: A siege in 701 BC	// 36:1–3 (some variants)	x
18:14–16: Hezekiah pays tribute	x	Hezekiah sends (large) tribute
18:19–37: The threat of the Rabshakeh	// 36:4–22	x
19:1–7: Hezekiah and Isaiah's response	// 37:1–7	x
19:8–13: The Rabshakeh returns	// 37:8–13	x
19:14–19: Hezekiah's prayer	// 37:14–20 (with minor variations)	x
19:20–34: Isaiah's prophecy	// 37:21–35	x
19:35–37: The angel of the Lord	// 37:36–38	Alternative ending: Sennacherib "departs for Nineveh"
"x" indicates that this part of the story is absent.		

Readers who read Isaiah only, note, will miss the fact that 2 Kings 18 "admitted" that Hezekiah paid an enormous tribute, as Sennacherib's account confirms (though the amounts are lower in the Kings version). Readers of Sennacherib's annals, on the other hand, will miss a great deal more . . .

Space permits only two brief comments at this point. First, Isaiah's agenda does not seem to be to give simply a historical account of the event, but rather to highlight how, in comparison to Ahaz's failure to "stand firm in faith" in chapter 7, here Hezekiah models exactly how a king *should* take to heart the word of a prophet at a crucial time. The payment of tribute does not contribute to this point, so is omitted. We can hardly understand these texts without situating them properly in their historical context, but the *focus* of the text is rarely a historical one, or simply a desire to give an account of what happened. There is always some bigger, theological agenda.

Secondly, we can extend this observation by noting that the agenda of the book of Isaiah is not even the same as that of 2 Kings. So how does the story go on in Isaiah? In chapter 38 Hezekiah becomes sick, but is reprieved, but then his tale comes to a striking end in chapter 39. Here he willingly shows some envoys from a far country all around his storehouses, his armory, and in fact anything they would like to see. The prophet Isaiah is appalled. One can imagine him saying, "You showed them *what?*" and then arguing about where they came from. "Well," says Hezekiah, "it was miles away, never heard of it in fact, some place called Babylon . . ." Historically Hezekiah might have been right that this was some remote nation hardly to be worried about. But the book of Isaiah leaves the tale there, hanging, suggesting to the reader that just because you might have dealt with the Assyrian threat does not mean that all will live happily ever after. The book is about to offer the editorial jump-cut to end all editorial cuts: chapter 40 will roll in at the end of a *Babylonian* exile, around a century and a half later, with its unforgettable "Comfort, O comfort my people . . . ," because Jerusalem's penalty *at the hand of the Babylonians* is almost paid for (40:2). Little if any of this is directly in view in the way the story is told in 2 Kings.

THE LITERARY FOCUS PROVIDED BY ISAIAH 1

Isaiah 1 seems to many scholars to provide an introduction to the whole book. Like most good introductions, this probably means it was one of the last bits written, but our point is rather that in reading Isaiah 1 today we might want to ask literary questions: How does this anticipate key themes? What does it set us up to look for?

Verse 1 packs in a list of kings and locations, but also tells us that we are about to read of "the vision (*chazon*) of Isaiah ben Amoz", the eighth century prophet often called "Isaiah of Jerusalem." In fact, chapter 2 will also begin with reference to "the word that Isaiah ben Amoz saw (*chazah*)." Quite how a prophet *sees* a *word* might help us to think about the idea of "grasping" what God is getting at, which would not be a bad way to try and read Isaiah. But comparing 1:1 and 2:1 perhaps underlines the ways in which chapter 1 works as a kind of "literary overture."

1:1		Introduction (or "superscription")	
1:2–31		Exhortation to Repentance	
	1:2–9		I. Divine Description of the Problem: Persistent Evil of Israel
	1:10–17		II. Divine Prescription of Solution: Call to Repentance
	1:18–31		III. Divine Argument for Participating in Solution: Outline of Consequences of Different Responses to II
2:1		Conclusion? (or new "superscription"?)	

Figure 4. Isaiah 1: A Structural Outline[10]

Many key issues in Isaiah are brought to the fore here. Israel is sinful. In the image borrowed for Christmas stories, it is compared unfavorably in verse 3 with the "ox and donkey" by the crib. "Unlike a knowing donkey, Israel will starve to death by rejecting its master. What a way to begin a book of the Bible!"[11] Verse 7 may well relate to the desolation caused by the siege of 701 BC, which we already discussed, but note that this passage does not really require us to identify that event in order to grasp the point. Rather, the emphasis is that Israel will suffer destruction from the Lord, unless it radically changes its ways. Thus 1:12–15 shows how it will be pointless if they carry on in their standard (apparently worshipping) ways without addressing the sin in the midst of them, while 1:16–17 lists nine ways in which they might seek to do something about it.

The judgment is not set arbitrarily. Verse 18 invites Israel to see God's logic: sin will reap its reward, while repentance will allow restoration. But then the chapter seems to cover a whole range of possibilities all at once. Jerusalem, of all places, is found wanting (verse 21). God's wrath will be poured out (verses 24–25). But "Zion shall be redeemed

10. There are different ways one could chart Isaiah 1. This one is drawn from Carr, "Reading Isaiah," 199.

11. Brueggemann, *Isaiah 1–39*, 13.

by justice" (verse 27). One might conceivably disentangle this as a historical narrative, though it is difficult to know who would have said this and when during the events described in the book, especially if we note the occasional word like "afterward" in 1:26. But more significantly, this passage stands as a kind of opening overview of the fundamental issue: how God's justice is or is not found mirrored in the lives of the people of God, and what will (or will not) happen as a result. Later chapters in the book that look at first sight as if they are simply oracles indiscriminately announcing judgment need to be read in the light of the kind of context set up here for the whole book. It is a stunning literary opening: "Isaiah 1 as a whole can be seen as a repentance-focused presentation of many central themes of the Isaiah tradition."[12]

Perhaps we may summarize it this way: What you are about to read, says Isaiah 1, is the long and complex tale of how God deals with his people, through their sins, their repentance, their insights, their stubbornness, and in and out of their land, of life, of hope. This has happened down through the centuries. It will continue to happen. Hear this word of the prophet. Or better: See it! Grasp the ways of God with his people. And to do so . . . go on and read the rest of the book.

THE CANONICAL FOCUS PROVIDED BY ISAIAH 6

Many people have heard the story of Isaiah 6. Verses 1–8 are read in the ordination services of many church traditions. Calls for missionary workers have long dwelt on the "who will go?/here I am—send me!" dynamic of the passage. It is powerful and moving imagery. It also gets deeply puzzling in verses 9–10 with a passage picked up in the Gospels and applied to Jesus, where Isaiah seems to be commissioned to a task of making people not understand unless they might turn and be healed. What is going on?

A canonical approach to this passage first of all notes that it is not chapter 1. In other words, it does not stand as a "call narrative" of the prophet at the beginning of the book, in the way that for example Jeremiah 1 relates the call of the prophet Jeremiah. Presumably there is something in Isaiah 1–5 which builds up to this text, and sets a scene for it. In addition to what we already saw in Isaiah 1, two brief observations about chapter 5 may be helpful here.

---

12. Carr, "Reading Isaiah," 203.

First, 5:7b carries a careful wordplay, literally:

> He expected justice (*mishpat*)/ but behold: bloodshed (*mispach*)
> Righteousness (*tsedaqah*)/ but behold: a cry! (*tse'aqah*)

The wordpair "justice and righteousness" occurs frequently in Isaiah especially, as a kind of banner-headline for the notion of a society founded on these core ways of living which seek the good for all. Just where one might expect to find these qualities most manifest—in "the vineyard of the Lord of hosts" as 5:7a puts it—there is instead a perversion of them. Then secondly, as chapter 5 wends its way through a list of six "woes" with which God afflicts Israel,[13] we build up to a picture of the lights going out (verse 30) and "only darkness and distress." It is as if the nation has lost its way completely. In which context, Isaiah's experience of the holy God is related: his lips burn, he is unclean, the temple shakes . . . God will not accept Israel's ways of "darkness" any longer. The prophet is to announce that the judgment is come.

There are other ways to read Isaiah 6, as there are other ways to read any deeply challenging passage of scripture. In this case, though, this "canonical" approach seems to gain support from noting that Isaiah's response is not, "I don't believe it," nor is it, "How can you ask such a thing?" but rather he says, "How long, O Lord?" (verse 11).[14] The answer is "Until . . ." (verses 11–13). In the context of the book of Isaiah, that "until" hangs over everything that follows. It hangs heavy in the air as the long-delayed seventh woe finally falls in 10:5, revealing, extraordinarily, that Assyria might even be understood as "the rod of [the Lord's] anger" as that particular oracle puts it. And it casts its gloom over much of the succeeding book right up to the long-delayed "Comfort, O comfort" of chapter 40. This kind of approach is asking: how can we make sense of a text in its particular location in the overall canonical narrative?

The various examples in this chapter of how to read Isaiah wisely have sought to show that (a) different approaches unlock different but valuable aspects of different biblical texts and (b) that we can understand certain key passages in the book quite well without knowing everything about the whole sixty-six chapters. Good news, I suspect, for those of us struggling to keep up with the great prophet Isaiah.

13. Isaiah 5:8, 11, 18, 20, 21, 22, translated "woe" in the NIV but as the somewhat enigmatic "ah" in the NRSV.

14. See here especially Seitz, *Isaiah 1–39*, 57.

PART TWO

Thinking Theologically about Scripture

6

The Inspiration of Scripture and the Breath of God

2 TIMOTHY 3:16; 2 PETER 1:20–21

S o far we have been discussing how to interpret biblical texts, and have been trying to let scripture itself be a guide for how we might go about that task. Theological questions have been among various other types of question we have been asking. It is time now to focus specifically on theological questions about the nature of scripture itself. This could lead us on to all sorts of topics, but we will limit ourselves to a few key areas, often understood as aspects of a "doctrine of scripture." Again, we shall consider specific verses and passages of scripture as a way in to the issues.

We begin with the notion of the "inspiration" of scripture. Discussion of this topic must inevitably at some point consider the well-known verse in 2 Timothy 3 that uses the word "inspiration." In fact, we shall suggest that this passage is rather less useful than another one in 2 Peter for understanding what is really at issue in describing the Bible as "inspired," but since it is a well-known focal point for our topic, we shall begin with it.

2 TIMOTHY 3:16

2 Timothy 3:16 occurs in a short passage in which Paul is writing to Timothy about various matters concerning how he might live an

appropriate life when under pressure, in the face of persecution.[1] Paul's answer: scripture offers the resource he needs. Here is the verse itself, from the NRSV translation, although on this occasion we will need to explore the translation quite carefully: "All scripture is inspired by God and is useful for teaching, for reproof, for correction, and for training in righteousness."

The structure of the verse seems clear. Two things are said about scripture: that it is inspired and that it is useful. What it is useful for is also clear: four different activities, although generally when people make a list of four activities they are seldom saying "four and only these four" but rather giving an illustrative list. Thus this may be an account of the kinds of things scripture is useful for. Nevertheless all the listed uses gravitate around the idea of instruction in Christian living.

The word translated "inspired" is the Greek word *theopneustos*, which occurs only here in the Bible. The word can in this instance be broken down into its component parts: *theos* (God), and *pneustos* (an adjective from the verb *pneō*—"to breathe," a verb related to the noun *pneuma*, the "spirit" or "breath"). Words cannot always be treated this way, as is obvious from trying to analyze "butterfly" into butter that flies, but in this case it works. This leaves us with "God-breathed" as a good translation for 2 Timothy 3:16: all scripture is God-breathed, which is in fact how the NIV translates this part of the verse. "Inspired" is the traditional word used in English, and while it does perhaps have a technical sense of "breathed into," in itself it misses out the fact that it is God who is doing the breathing. It also raises the interesting question of whether God is breathing *into* scripture or whether we would be better off saying that God breathes *out* of it, or through it. The difference is perhaps between a book into which God breathes his spirit, or a book which is itself breathed out as the breath of God. It has on occasion been suggested that we could call scripture "*ex*-spired" by God in order to capture precisely this nuance of meaning, but given the way this would sound when spoken out loud ("scripture is expired!") this is unlikely to catch on.

We said above that we would need to examine the translation quite carefully. In the 1960s the New English Bible (NEB) caused quite a stir by offering a different interpretation of the verse. Due to a certain flexibility

---

1. New Testament scholars are often of the opinion that Paul did not in fact write 2 Timothy. This not particularly interesting question need not occupy us here. We shall call the author "Paul" for the sake of simplicity.

in the wording of the Greek, there is actually a possible ambiguity in the phrase "all scripture." Although the verse can indeed be translated "all scripture is inspired," as per the traditional view, the NEB opted for an alternative wording: "Every inspired scripture has its use for . . ."[2] Clearly this latter option might suggest that only those parts of scripture which are inspired are useful, opening up the possibility that only selected parts of scripture are inspired. There are a range of separate issues here. Let us pause for a moment and look more closely at the passage, including the previous verse:

> [15] . . . from childhood you have known the sacred writings (*hiera grammata*—"holy writings") that are able to instruct you for salvation through faith in Christ Jesus. [16] All scripture (*graphē*—literally "writing, text") is inspired by God and is useful . . . (2 Timothy 3:15–16)

One possibility is that verse 16 is actually picking out "scripture" from the more general category of "holy writings." In that sense, "all inspired scripture" is nothing other than a way of picking out the appropriate group of texts. Furthermore, "all scripture"—a singular term rather than a plural one—may very well mean "every (instance of) scripture," or in other words "every scriptural text." On a case-by-case basis, Paul may be saying, whenever you have scripture, you have something useful. Perhaps the two alternative translations are not as far apart as they might have first seemed. On the other hand, it does seem just as (if not more) likely that the traditional interpretation is appropriate. But the reasons behind the majority view are not grammatical—they are conceptual. It is of course *possible* that Paul was saying that only the inspired parts of scripture are useful. However, this would have been quite a startling claim, since it would have been generally assumed that scripture was inspired. The argument therefore runs that if Paul had wanted to make a case for "partial inspiration" then it would have required something more than a passing reference. This is evidently not a conclusive argument, but as we shall see in this chapter more than once, conclusive arguments are not exactly in abundance when it comes to a doctrine of inspiration. We shall therefore continue with the traditional rendering of the verse, as quoted above.

2. The NEB contained many oddities, most of which were either quietly removed or dramatically improved in its revision, the Revised English Bible (REB) in 1989. This one, however, it retained as "All inspired scripture has its use . . ."

However, this discussion does illuminate one important point. Paul's reference to "inspiration" is really a passing reference. This is not an occasion on which he chooses to lay out his understanding of what might be meant by the word. He does clarify it a little, with the fourfold description of usefulness, but again only in passing. The question that follows from this is to ask what he *is* really talking about if this is not his topic as such. We therefore need to ask about the context of this verse. It is all very well to quote it as a freestanding point about the inspiration of scripture, but why did Paul say it? Was he engaged in the task of setting up just such a doctrine? No he was not.

As we already noted, the context of the verse in 2 Timothy 3:10–17 demonstrates that Paul's concern is to encourage Timothy in the godly lifestyle which he has been pursuing. Timothy is exhorted to "continue in what you have learned and firmly believed" (verse 14), and reminded that one of the resources for just such a continuation is the scriptures that he has known since childhood. Thus Timothy is to continue to let his life be shaped and molded by the scriptures he has already been working with, knowing then that these scriptures come with the imprint of the very breath of God. The goal, in verse 17, is that "the man of God" might be equipped for every good work. Some translations, including the NRSV, generalize this to "everyone," partly to avoid the gender-exclusive language of "man of God." Others conclude that Paul said "man" to refer more specifically to a (male) leader of a congregation, or arguably to Timothy himself, and they leave the translation as "man of God." Whichever of these is right, today's readers may rightly conclude that the profitability of scripture is secure for all who wish to live godly lives, male or female.

This is as practical a context as one could wish to find for reflecting on the use of scripture, and it touches on the nature of scripture only in the clarity with which it makes its practical point. This is doubtless why Paul does not define what he means by "inspiration." It is also one reason why, in the end, this verse will make only a limited contribution to an understanding of a Christian doctrine of the inspiration of scripture. On the whole, it seems best to work with the passage on its own terms and leave our understanding of inspiration at the relatively general level of "God-breathed for practical purposes (i.e., teaching, training in righteousness, and so forth)."

One further point follows on from this one, and takes us into a particular detail about how the "inspiration" of the biblical text is to be understood. It is sometimes said that the "inspiration" of scripture is a characteristic of only the "original manuscripts"—in other words the texts as they were originally written down (in Hebrew and Greek), but not as they were subsequently copied. Here we need to know something of the mechanism by which the biblical text has been passed on from its original writing through to its preservation in later Hebrew and Greek copies, and then on into translation. When Paul wrote a letter, and if it was thought worthy of wider circulation, for example among the various churches of the time, it would be copied out for this purpose. Inevitably, over time, variations would creep in between different copies. In so far as we have a variety of ancient versions of any biblical book, this is still a relevant point today when an edition of the Bible has to choose between alternative copies, or "readings."

Giving attention to this issue is the work of "textual criticism." The resulting various possibilities for some verses occupy the footnotes of different Bible translations, and on the whole indicate that we are talking about relatively minor matters and particular details when we are weighing up the differences between different copies of the originals. To give one illustration: the verb about knees "bowing" in Philippians 2:10 has two different spellings in different texts, representing two different nuances of what it might be saying. In one case it is saying "that every knee will bow," and in the other "that every knee could (or might) bow," with the one reading suggesting that all will one day voluntarily worship God, while in the other the bowing may be more of a forced acknowledgement. This particular case does not usually merit a footnote in English translations, but it ties in a quotation of Isaiah 45:23, the question of whether Philippians 2 contains a "hymn" which Paul is quoting, and a point of theology about the final state of all people before God. This kind of example shows how many interlinked questions there often are from any one verse of scripture. In our present context it also raises the question: which of these two readings is "inspired?"

This question, or at least questions like it, is widely asked at the more conservative end of the theological spectrum, but it also reflects a modern tendency across the whole range of theological views to seek the earliest possible meaning of a text as in some sense definitive, whether of what the author intended, or what the text meant, or means. The tendency is

to pursue the earliest text as the one that God "inspired," with later altera-
tions reflecting deviations or corruptions away from the pure norm. This
view of life is indeed something of a modern phenomenon, and it is ill-
equipped to deal with the biblical text that we actually have.

There are perhaps biblical books where there was one definitive author's version of the complete work. Philemon might be a good candidate
for this status. But more often there is not any necessity to imagine one
fixed first text. With a book such as Acts, for instance, there are at least
two different (if usually overlapping) versions of the text in circulation,
known as the "Western" and the "Eastern" texts. The book of Jeremiah,
to take a more striking example, exists in two quite substantially different traditions, which include whole sections of Jeremiah's oracles
in different orders. On the whole these issues do not much trouble the
mainstream of theological tradition. More specifically, what they really
do is undermine the whole approach of saying that a characteristic of
"biblical inspiration" can be said to apply to some "original manuscript"
in a way in which it does not apply to later copies of the text.[3]

By coming back to 2 Timothy 3, we may go further. Here the scriptures which are described as *theopneustos* are the ones Timothy has
known and been using since his childhood. These would be the scriptures of the Old Testament. In fact they would be the Greek translation
of the Old Testament, the Septuagint, which his mother and grandmoth-
er presumably read to him (1:4; 3:14). Thus insofar as 2 Timothy 3:16
bears on any doctrine of inspiration, the conclusion is quite striking.
The scripture, which turns out to be useful for teaching, training, and
so forth is a translation—and it is this translation which is described
as "inspired." Thus this passage actually opposes the idea that biblical
inspiration should be thought of as applying to the original manuscripts.
It requires instead that it apply to the version of the scriptures accepted
into use by the church. From the modern perspective, with its liking for
both accuracy and originality, this may seem a little vague. However, we
should accept that this is not the way it looked for most of church history. We might also draw some comfort from this point, if we are among
those who read the Bible in English, for example. It would be a strange
idea of "inspiration" if in practice no one alive today had ever read an
inspired Bible. But that would be the case if it were only the original
manuscripts which were inspired. Instead, if translations can indeed

---

3. See further the useful brief discussion of Beckwith, "Biblical Text."

count as inspired, then this is good news: those who have read the Bible in their own language have still been reading the inspired book.[4]

2 PETER 1:20–21

The discussion so far has circled around 2 Timothy 3:16 with enough of a view of its context to allow us to begin to formulate a doctrine of the inspiration of scripture. However, despite the prominence given to 2 Timothy 3:16 in discussions of our topic, my own view is that a short passage in 2 Peter 1 is actually more helpful for understanding what is at stake in the idea.

Peter's letters offer two insights (at least) into how the Spirit is at work in and through our human efforts to interpret. There is a fascinating passage in 1 Peter 1:10–12, where he makes the claim that the Spirit of Christ within the (presumably Old Testament) prophets enabled them to serve Peter's own listeners, by testifying "in advance to the sufferings destined for Christ and the subsequent glory" (verse 11). This passage would certainly help us think through many matters of scripture, although it does not directly address our current topic of inspiration.[5]

Our main focus, therefore, will be on 2 Peter 1:19–21. The claim which begins the build-up to this passage is found in verse 16: the "power and coming" (*dynamis* and *parousia*) of "our Lord Jesus Christ" are not myths or stories, he says, using "stories" here in a negative sense of accounts made up by people who should not be trusted. Rather, in this case, Peter affirms that there are two reasons why his readers can trust these particular claims. The first is that both he and his audience were "eyewitnesses of his [Jesus'] majesty" on the mount of transfiguration. In other words, their experience during Jesus' life on earth should demonstrate to them now the certainty of Jesus' "power and coming." The second reason brings us to the role of scripture, again referring to what we would now call the Old Testament. In fact he is more specific: it

4. We cannot discuss the many questions of detail which might arise at this point. For a thought-provoking account of how one might go further, see Chapman, "Inspiration."

5. Note Green, *1 Peter*, 251, who suggests that 1 Peter 1:10–12 offers a programmatic statement of "a theological hermeneutic of scripture": in other words Christ is the key to the unity of Old Testament expectation and New Testament fulfillment in a pattern already found in the Old Testament scriptures, rather than just being read back from the New.

is the word (or message; *logos*) of the prophets that is in view. What does Peter say about this?

First he says it is now "fully confirmed." It was always sure, but he and they now have additional reason to trust it, in the light of what they have seen. Secondly, it demands attention, like a light shining in a dark place. He says more on this, but we must move on to the key point for our discussion. That arrives in verse 20, which says literally that "every prophecy of scripture does not come of its own interpretation." This sentence could mean a range of things. The NRSV opts for "no prophecy of scripture is a matter of one's own interpretation," and the NIV gives us "no prophecy of Scripture came about by the prophet's own interpretation." These two understandings leave the emphasis on the recipient and the giver of the prophetic message (*logos*) respectively. It is hard to know which is correct, but perhaps in the context there may be a slight reason to prefer the NIV translation, which underlines the point that the prophets did not make things up when they prophesied.

The key is that when prophets spoke, it was not just them speaking, but God too. Verse 21 is explicit: "no prophecy ever came by human will, but men and women moved by the Holy Spirit spoke from God." This is the heart of the matter. The prophets spoke because they were "moved by the Holy Spirit." There is no particular word here which one might translate as "inspired," such as there was in 2 Timothy 3, but clearly the idea of inspiration is precisely what is at stake.

In fact, this idea is probably more commonly what is in mind when people talk of the inspiration of the Bible than anything we found in 2 Timothy 3 (except the word "inspired" itself). Peter emphasizes that human will and divine will were somehow working as one. In the history of the church there have been various theories to explain how this might have been so, ranging from a "dictation" view at one extreme (where God "dictated" the words to the prophet who simply took them down) right through to a vague sense of God giving someone a great idea which they then wrote up in their own time, at the other extreme.[6] Somewhere in the middle of that spectrum we would be in the right place: the prophetic word was the work of the prophet, and indeed prophetic oracles do seem to reflect the style and personality of the individual prophet concerned, but it was also, *at the same time*, the work of God.

---

6. For a helpful survey of this "spectrum" see Bloesch, *Holy Scripture*, 85–130.

A doctrine of inspiration should probably be saying something like that about the biblical text. The text is both the words of the human author, and in and through that it is the word brought by God too. It is only fair to point out that this idea, found in 2 Peter 1, referred in the first instance only to "the word of the prophets," rather than to every kind of scriptural text. Certainly it seems more straightforward to see how this works for a prophecy than for a collection of wisdom literature, or a genealogy, for example. However, we should probably not over-press this point. It may be that "prophecy" was something of a general term for much of scripture at the time—recall an earlier chapter where we looked at the "law and the prophets" as the scripture upon which Jesus drew. Although we should not say that 2 Peter 1 is simply talking about any kind of scriptural text, I suggest that we are not led astray if we extrapolate his thinking about prophecy to our own thinking about scripture. We will return to this point at the conclusion of the chapter.

SCRIPTURAL TEXTS AND A DOCTRINE OF SCRIPTURE

The two passages we have discussed are the most important New Testament ones for our purposes. There are some others that deserve a brief comment too, although none of them are directly about inspiration. However, insofar as such verses might shed light on the nature or purpose of scripture, they may be indirectly relevant. We will consider briefly only one of them. Again the conclusions will be limited: negative in the sense that we need caution in drawing conclusions about what exactly a notion of "inspiration" commits us to.

John 10:35 has Jesus saying "the scripture cannot be annulled" (or "broken", as the NIV puts it). This perhaps suggests a kind of guaranteed success in the attainment of scripture's goals or intended effects. In fact, this verse is a(nother) good example of a verse which needs to be read carefully in context. Jesus is arguing with "the Jews," who in John's Gospel, we have to assume, are not Jewish people in general, but some particular section of the Jewish people—perhaps leaders in Jerusalem at the time—who are the subjects of some of the most damning characterization in the entire Bible.[7] These Jews are accusing Jesus of blasphemy since he has just said "the Father and I are one." What clearer indication

7. Most notoriously in John 8:44. On this difficult issue see the helpful overview of Motyer, *Antisemitism.*

could they need of the fact that Jesus sees himself as equal in some sense with God? Jesus' response is that their own law says, "you are gods," speaking of those to whom the word of God came, in Psalm 82:6. This Psalm imagines God in his rightful place as ruler of a "divine council" of other gods, an idea well enough known in the time of the Psalms, and in the surrounding nations, but one that might be a little problematic to us today if we were to take it as a literal description of how we see God's role in the universe. Nevertheless, it is this Psalm which prompts Jesus to say that "the scripture cannot be broken." Does Jesus really believe that Psalm 82 is a depiction of the way the world is? What seems more likely is that he is conducting an argument against those Jews who are accusing him, pointing out that—according to their own way of looking at things—the scripture cannot be broken, and that they are therefore ill-placed to accuse him of exactly what Psalm 82 says is true of anyone to whom the word of God came. Perhaps John thought this was a good argument, which may be why it turns up in his gospel. Perhaps he is just recording the incident. Either way, John 10:35 offers little evidence that scripture's divine origin ensures that it is incapable of failing in its aim. Such a view is usually related to the notion of the "infallibility" of scripture—literally, that scripture does not "fail." Of course, one would have to know what it was trying to do in order to judge whether it had succeeded or failed. It is worth noting that the more common range of terms scripture itself applies to the word of God is "trustworthy," and hence by implication "reliable." Whether or not this makes it incapable of failure may not be the most helpful discussion to pursue.

There is one final point to make in this chapter, and it may have been nagging at some readers throughout. Surely this has all been an exercise in circular reasoning? How could one base a doctrine of scrip-ture on what scripture itself says? Obviously that would indeed be a circular argument. I have no interest in trying to argue the impossible case that "we must believe X about the Bible because the Bible itself says X." The goal is more limited. Furthermore, almost always when the New Testament talks about "scripture" it is, as we have noted several times in this chapter, talking about the Old Testament. This is another reason why we cannot simply lift our doctrine of scripture out of individual biblical verses. So what can we say?

My own view is that we are not "basing" our doctrine on particular verses found here or there. Rather we are hoping that whenever verses here or there touch on our topic, the resulting insights will shape what it is we are trying to say with the doctrine. To be specific: we do not have our view of inspiration simply because of 2 Timothy 3 or 2 Peter 1, but whatever our view of inspiration is, it will be wiser if it takes on board the ways of thinking found in these passages. There should be a fit, in other words, between how the New Testament authors thought of scripture and how we do. There will of course be differences too, not least because we are trying to account for the New Testament. In the end, much of what we want to say about scripture will not fit into a doctrine of inspiration. But inspiration is one important aspect of what we should be saying.

In considering the inspiration of scripture we have been considering a biblical text filled with the spirit, or breath, of God. As a result, we may say that the Bible we have is the one that God was happy to leave with us—copying errors, grammatical problems, historical and ethical hard questions notwithstanding. The desire of some to turn the Bible into the book that they would have produced had they been in God's shoes, whether the "they" in question is on the left or the right of the theological spectrum, needs to be resisted.

We turn next to the related question of the "canon" of biblical books that we now have. In the process we shall see that this sheds some further light on our discussion of biblical inspiration.

7

The Canon of Scripture and the Rule of Faith

IT IS AN OBVIOUS point that if you held in your hands a copy of, say, 1 Corinthians, removed from its context as a New Testament book," you would not by looking at it be able to deduce that it was more than a letter. It would clearly look like what it is: Paul's letter to Corinth. It might stand out to you because it is theologically profound, or because you are a female prophet and a bit concerned about its contents, or for a whole variety of reasons. But it does not have a footnote: "inspired bit of the Bible." This raises the historical question so easily passed over by a lot of simplistic theories of inspiration: How did the early church recognize an inspired document when it saw one? Interestingly enough, the early church did not particularly think that God was inspiring the selection of a collection of books in the same way that God inspired the books themselves. So how did we end up with this particular collection of Bible books and not another?

The example of 1 Corinthians is obviously a New Testament one. It is slightly harder to give a comparable Old Testament example, if only because the Old Testament does not contain letters clearly written from one person to a particular situation at a particular time. But the overall point is the same: What led the people of God to have the particular collection of books in their holy scripture which they did, and not another? The shape of the answer to these two questions—regarding the Old and

New Testament canons—is similar in some ways but different in one important respect: that the New Testament developed in a situation which already had a pre-existing canon of scripture before it. We shall see how this makes a difference as we proceed.

One other brief point may be made first, regarding the word "canon" itself. The word comes from the Greek *kanōn*, which was originally the word for a strong tall reed such as might have grown by a river. Break it off and you could use it to measure things, and see whose camel was taller than whose. Thus the "reed" became a measuring rod. From there the word developed the sense of a norm or a standard. In fact it is used in this way in Galatians 6:16: "as for those who follow this *rule* (*kanōn*) . . ." The key point, to which we shall return later, is that there is then a double sense of the word, to refer both to the standard (all the camels three reeds high, for example) and all those things that meet the standard (the list of camels themselves). Applied to books rather than camels, we have the makings of "the biblical canon." But we are getting ahead of ourselves.

THE OLD TESTAMENT CANON

There are thirty-nine books in the standard Protestant Old Testament. They match the books that make up Jewish scripture, although Jewish readers count them as only twenty-four books. We shall set to one side for a moment the higher figure that we find in Roman Catholic Bibles. In traditional Protestant Bibles the thirty-nine books of the Old Testament are arranged into four main sections: Law, Histories, Poetry and Wisdom, Prophets. This is not the traditional order of the Hebrew canon, which is laid out in the box below.

The Old Testament—The 24 Books of the Hebrew Canon		
Torah *(torah)*	The Prophets *(nebi'im)*	
Genesis Exodus Leviticus Numbers Deuteronomy	*Former Prophets:* Joshua Judges Samuel Kings	*Latter Prophets:* Isaiah Jeremiah Ezekiel The Book of the Twelve
The Writings *(ketubim)*		
Psalms Job Proverbs	*The 5 Scrolls: (Megilloth)* Ruth Song of Songs Ecclesiastes Lamentations Esther	Daniel Ezra–Nehemiah Chronicles

Fig 5. The Hebrew Canon

The initial letters of the three Hebrew words for the three main sections of scripture, listed in the above chart, give us a name for the Hebrew scriptures: *t-n-k*, usually pronounced *tanakh*. This serves as one possible name for the book in Hebrew. Jewish translations of scripture may be bought as "The Tanakh" in bookstores.

The Hebrew order sets the Torah apart as the primary section, divides the "Prophets" into "Former" and "Latter," and groups everything else together as "Writings." This "writings" section is also divided into three, though these divisions are less significant: the Psalms and other poetic writings first; then the "Five Scrolls," traditionally each read at a festival during the worshipping year, and finally the latest books, offering a kind of review and overview from the end of the Old Testament age.

The study of the Old Testament canon has developed hugely over the past few years.[1] It is interesting to read the Old Testament with the Hebrew canon in mind, because it represents an understanding of the texts more closely allied to their original contexts. But there are limitations to this approach, if we are interested in reading the Old Testament as Christian scripture. Nevertheless, before exploring what difference that makes, it is helpful to be reminded that a book like Samuel was

1. See Barton, *Christian Bible*, for a clear introduction to this topic.

understood as "prophetic," presumably because it brought a word from God, or that the five books of the Torah were a foundation for Israel's scripture, perhaps rather like the gospels operate in the New Testament.

The location and identification of the "Prophets" illuminates some of the key differences between reading these texts in their Jewish and then their Christian contexts. The next chart tries to highlight the points of similarity and of difference:

Old Testament Prophetic Literature				
Hebrew Canon		*Christian (Protestant) Canon*		
3 parts	Torah (*torah*) [5] Prophets (*nebi'im*) [8] Writings (*ketubim*) [11]	4 parts	Pentateuch [5] History [12] Poetic & Wisdom books [5] Prophets [17]	
No. of books	24	No. of books	39	
Prophets come after the Torah: they interpret the Torah for the on-going life of God's people		Prophets come before the New Testament: they point forward to Jesus and the coming of the Spirit		
Prophets in 2 parts:	Former Prophets Latter Prophets	Prophets in 2 parts:	Major Prophets Minor Prophets	
Former Prophets: Joshua Judges Samuel Kings	*Latter Prophets:* Isaiah Jeremiah Ezekiel The Twelve	*Major Prophets:* Isaiah Jeremiah Lamentations Ezekiel Daniel	*Minor Prophets:*	
			Hosea Joel Amos Obadiah Jonah Micah	Nahum Habakkuk Zephaniah Haggai Zechariah Malachi

Fig 6. The Prophets in the Jewish and Christian Canons

The difference in the number of books arises because Jewish tradition treats several texts as single books where the Christian tradition splits them into two halves (Samuel, Kings, and Chronicles, as well as Ezra–Nehemiah), and something similar happens with the "Book of the Twelve," which counts for twelve books in the Christian Bible. Some have suggested that these shorter books were indeed intended to be read as part of a longer sequence, or whole, where each "Minor Prophet" picks up themes of other ones and leaves certain questions hanging for the next one. These kinds of observations occupy those who read the books "canonically," which we considered in earlier chapters as an important theological angle for reading biblical texts.

The classification of prophets has certain interesting features. Daniel is not a book of the prophets in the Hebrew canon, although Daniel himself was understood as a prophet in the time of Jesus, as Jesus himself attests (Matt 24:15//Mark 13:14). Some argue that Daniel would have been a prophetic book but that it came too late for inclusion in the second section of the canon. Others say that the reason for its position is more to do with its unusual contents, and that there was no fixed point at which the "Prophets" were separated off from the "Writings." We looked in chapter 1 above at Luke 24, where Jesus was interpreting "Moses and the prophets," and we suggested that this was a way of pointing to all of scripture at the time. In fact Luke 24:44 has an unusual reference to "the law of Moses, the prophets, and the psalms," which could indicate something more like the threefold division which we have been looking at here. In which case, Jesus is specifically referring to three-fold scripture in Luke 24:44 as "fulfilled in me." It is debated exactly how the division into sections of scripture was understood and when. Less debated, though also far less significant, is the observation that the labels "Major" and "Minor" come from the Latin words indicating larger and smaller. These descriptions of the prophetic books refer solely to their length, and not their significance.

Theologically, we may say that the Torah is at the heart of Jewish scripture. It sets the standard around which the other books gather. In Jewish thinking, it is natural then to see the prophets as interpreting the Torah. The prophetic task could be seen as being to call God's people— and less often other people—to live lives which measured up to the standards set out in the Torah. Even if that is not true historically in terms of when individual books were written down, it does make sense today as a way of reading Jewish scripture.

When we look at the prophets in the Christian Bible, though, they have been moved to the end to point forward to the coming of Christ. This highlights their predictive prophecies, especially the messianic ones. It brings out quite strongly the way in which prophets looked ahead to the future. Sometimes people contrast these two different approaches, and suggest that we should go back to the more "ethical" emphasis of the Jewish understanding if we really want to get the prophets right.

However, perhaps we should rather say that there are (at least) two sides to the prophetic message of these prophets, and both have their place.

It is not a coincidence that the Christian arrangement puts Malachi 4:4–6 at the very end of the Old Testament, looking back to Moses and Elijah (the law and the prophets?) and then looking forward to the "day of the Lord." In contrast, the Jewish canon ends with the final promise in the book of Chronicles, which is that the Israelites may return from exile and rebuild the temple (2 Chr 36:22–23). This is a wonderfully appropriate ending for temple-orientated worshipers of the God of Israel. Malachi is a wonderfully appropriate ending too, but in a different way. The question of where the two versions of the canon end is a specific example of how the canon sets the individual books into a larger context, which contributes to the way we are invited to read them.

This point is true too, though in a different way, for the books of the New Testament. Before turning to them, we should just say a very brief word about those extra books in the Catholic Bible which we set to one side at the beginning of our discussion: the "Apocrypha."

THE APOCRYPHA

The writing of important books did not stop after the final prophets mentioned above. The understanding of prophecy perhaps changed, and there was indeed a view amongst some in Israel that the prophetic voice had ceased.[2] Books, however, continued to be written. Some of the most important tended to be gathered together as an "addendum" to the canon. This led to a name for them: "deutero-canonical," meaning "of secondary canonical status." Many Bibles print these today between the Old and New Testaments. They tell us much about the period in between the testaments, either as historical accounts, or short stories, or wisdom writing.

The number of books involved is not easy to define. This is because some of them are in the form of "additions." In particular there are lengthy additions to the book of Esther, and a couple of delightful narratives added to the book of Daniel, known as "Susanna" and "Bel and the Dragon," which can also be printed as chapters 13 and 14 of

---

2. It is debated how widely this view was held, though verses such as 1 Maccabees 4:45–46 and 9:27 show that at least some thought this way. A good discussion of what can and cannot be said about this is offered by McDonald, *Biblical Canon*, 170–73.

Daniel itself. Aside from these additions, there are basically seven books: Tobit, Judith, Wisdom of Solomon, Ecclesiasticus,[3] Baruch (known from the book of Jeremiah as Jeremiah's scribe, and thus usually this book is printed along with Jeremiah), and two accounts of the period in 1 and 2 Maccabees, which we have mentioned in earlier chapters. The situation is further complicated by there being different listings of these books in different church traditions.

Why are they called "Apocrypha"? The word simply means "hidden (things)," and suggests that these books are hidden away, not to be read. In fact, it was probably Jerome (c. 345–420) who was responsible for setting them apart as "apocrypha," and he seemed to mean something more like "excluded from public worship." They were still worth reading for general interest and value. Historically speaking, the church then lived with a fairly vague view of the status of these books, for many centuries, hence the label "deutero-canonical." It was Martin Luther, in the sixteenth century, who insisted that they be removed from the canon, on various grounds (some of which were theologically motivated), but which he could express relatively straightforwardly by saying that they were not written in Hebrew, and were therefore not part of Hebrew scripture.[4] Luther's typically strong view provoked something of a counter-reaction, and the Catholic Church at this point insisted that they should be included. Thus after centuries in which there was no one definite view about them, there were suddenly two. The Anglican Church, taking its cue from Jerome, claims in its thirty-nine articles that these "other Books . . . the Church does read for example of life and instruction of manners; but yet it does not apply them to establish any doctrine."[5] This seems a suitably middle-ground way of dealing with the books.[6]

---

3. Also known as Ben Sira, or "The Wisdom of Jesus Son of Sirach."

4. In fact some of them were originally written in Hebrew, though the Hebrew copies were not available at the time of Luther. Hebrew copies of Ben Sira, for example, were only found at the end of the nineteenth century.

5. Article 6 of the thirty-nine articles. I have mildly updated the language from its 1571 English original (—the articles first appeared in Latin in 1563).

6. The interested reader will find a good account of the various books in Kaiser, *Old Testament Apocrypha*.

THE NEW TESTAMENT CANON

Many readers of the Bible today find themselves asking. "What do I do with the problematic Old Testament?" Such readers perhaps express a devotion to Jesus, but declare that they are troubled by, for example, "the angry God of the Old Testament." I am not going to address that particular question here, but am merely going to point out that for the very early Christians this "problem" was in fact exactly the opposite way around. They knew their God and their scriptures (our "Old Testament"), but the problem was what to make of Jesus. He seemed to sit light to Torah, and to make theologically problematic claims for those of orthodox convictions. In the words of Brevard Childs: "the problem of the early church was not what to do with the Old Testament in the light of the gospel, but rather the reverse."[7]

Recall that the "canon" of scripture is not just the list of what is in it, as if "canon" were a piece of theological jargon for "contents page." It was also the norm or standard by which the various books of scripture were understood to work together, for a common purpose. In the early church, the particular norm or standard which mattered was the "rule of faith" (which in Greek was *ho kanōn tēs pisteōs*: "the canon (or rule) of faith," also known by its Latin name, the *regula fidei*). This rule of faith was the "norm" or "standard" by which the church measured whether something has authority for its faith and life; in other words this was its canon. What was it?

To oversimplify a complex process, this "rule of faith" had to take on board the two main ways in which the early church now understood God to have spoken: through the scriptures (i.e., the "Old Testament," to use the anachronistic label), and through Christ. Exactly this kind of thinking is found at the beginning of the book of Hebrews: "Long ago God spoke to our ancestors in many and various ways by the prophets, but in these last days he has spoken to us by a Son . . ." (Hebrews 1:1–2). The two "words" of God, scripture and Christ, must have been a unity, since God was a unity, but how was Christ to be understood within this larger scriptural story? The way to try and bring these together was to construct a broad enough understanding to hold together the creator and redeemer God of the (Old Testament) scripture with the God who

---

7. Childs, *Church's Guide*, 61. He attributes this insight to von Campenhausen, *Christian Bible*, 64–65.

had now acted among them in Jesus. The resultant understanding, or its standard or measure, was the "canon" of faith: the rule of faith.

The rule of faith was never defined in an official set of words, such as the manner in which the early creeds were formulated. The phrase appears to have been loosely derived from Romans 12:3, where Paul urges that we think of ourselves appropriately, "according to the measure of faith" which God has given us. "Measure" here is *metron*, from which we get the ideas of metric, meter, and so forth, but the idea is the same as saying that there is a norm or standard of faith. In so far as this is found in a collection of writings, then, the church comes to say that its "canon" is its collection of writings. Thus, in a long process, but definitely by the middle of the fourth century, the "canon" exists both as a list of writings—the now two testament Bible—and as an authoritative measure built into those writings.

It is important to grasp at least the outlines of this argument historically. Many factors went into the adoption of a (New Testament) text as part of this canon, and the New Testament canon thus always had an in-built theological "standard" which ensured that what was in it was useful for faith and life. Note that there never was a period when the church existed when it did not have scripture: it had the Torah, the Prophets, and the Writings from before day one. But as it added further writings, it was developing them around its central convictions about who God was and what God had done.

It would be straightforward, perhaps, if we could cite some early church authority explaining exactly what the criteria were for knowing whether a book fitted with this understanding. We cannot do that. In a modern equivalent, the American theologian David Kelsey once attempted to pin down the questions of the criteria and framework regarding the differing uses of Scripture, and resorted to the memorable phrase that it was: "what 'the Christian thing' is basically all about."[8] I have come to think that this inelegant expression is actually a very helpful phrase, because it indicates both that we know what we are talking about ("what it is all about"), and also that we struggle to express it in clear terms (it is "the Christian thing"). A philosopher might say that we are

---

8. Kelsey, "Bible and Christian Theology," 385. See more generally his *Proving Doctrine*.

looking for books that have "family resemblances" between them: we know them when we see them, but do not ask us to define them.[9]

Can we say any more than that? We can indeed indicate some of the factors involved in the early church's decisions about whether a book or writing was to be understood as measuring up to the "canon," or in other words "canonical." They looked for whether it was written by or derived from an apostle, so that for example Mark's Gospel was said to be developed from the apostle Peter's recollections. They considered whether a writing had relevance beyond its original setting, noting that Paul's letters had something to say to a wider audience than just the original intended audience in Corinth or wherever. They tried to measure whether a writing was theologically orthodox—according to the faith already revealed in (Old Testament) scripture, for example. They wanted to know whether it had some kind of track record in being used constructively in Christian living and worship in some of the various churches that were growing up. Finally, was it "inspired" by God? Arguably we might have thought, at first, that this last criterion would have been the key. But as we saw in the last chapter, and now differently in this one, you could not tell just by looking at a piece of writing that it was "inspired" apart from weighing up these various other factors, and measuring the writing up against the "canon" of faith. What we see is that these different factors cannot all be separated out and analyzed one by one, but that they work together and demonstrate over time that a book was to play an ongoing role in the Christian faith.

This "vagueness" about exactly whether a book measured up to the "canon" standard or not should suggest that there would have been some debate about whether particular books did or did not measure up. In fact this is what we do find if we investigate this issue. The question of whether 2 Peter or Jude should be included went on for ages. As late as the Reformation prominent theologians were lamenting the fact that Revelation ever got in and whether it was really too late to do something about it. In the third and fourth centuries there was some variation concerning the later books in the New Testament as to whether they were in or not. It is worth pointing out that the Gospels and major Pauline letters were hardly if ever at stake, and this gives us a fairly solid and mainstream grasp of just what the theological standard is (or was) by which these other books were judged. The book of Jude appears to

---

9. That philosopher would be Ludwig Wittgenstein, but that is neither here nor there.

have got in because it was written by Jude, the brother of Jesus. That it quotes a lot of non-canonical sources in the course of its short and relatively unspectacular argument caused some concern, and appears to be why pretty much the entire argument of Jude reappears in 2 Peter 2, with all the non-scriptural references removed. It would be odd if one met someone for whom the inclusion of the book of Jude in the Bible has made the key difference in their growth in the Christian life. In fact not just odd, but slightly alarming too. Jude is not the heart of "what the Christian thing is all about," for all its merits, wisdom, and wonderful closing blessing, or "doxology" (Jude 24–25).

The evidence also demonstrates that quite a few books which in the end did not make it in to the canon were included at various times and places, such as the first epistle of Clement, or an apocalyptic work entitled *The Shepherd of Hermas*. A knowledge of these books is of great help in understanding early Christianity, and in the process can shed a lot of light on New Testament texts. But if one is abiding by the traditional decisions of the church, then there is no further scope for reading such texts "as Christian scripture."

This whole issue is not only a matter of historical interest. The discovery in 1945–46 of what is now known as *The Gospel of Thomas* at Nag Hammadi in Egypt, as part of a large "gnostic" library of texts dating back to the second century, raised the whole question again.[10] Should *Thomas* be included in the New Testament? Is it, as some scholars have argued, a fifth gospel, and thus to be published alongside the other four, as the "Jesus Seminar" in the United States has done?[11] How could we tell? *The Gospel of Thomas* is a short collection of 114 numbered sayings ranging from some which we also find in the canonical Gospels through to sayings which fall some way short of the tests of orthodoxy or "traditional usage." Just the last two sayings illustrate this very well: Thomas 113 is basically Luke 17:20–21. Jesus responds to a question about when the kingdom will come by saying that even while people say "Look here!" or "Look there!" it will not come that way, but it is spread out on the earth and people do not see it. In Thomas 114, however, Jesus responds to a comment that women are unworthy of "the Life" by saying

10. Gnosticism was an approach to faith that emphasized secret knowledge—"gnosis"—and although it is hinted at in various places in the New Testament, it only developed fully in the second century.

11. Funk and Hoover, *Five Gospels*.

that "every woman who makes herself male will enter the Kingdom of Heaven." End of gospel. Not quite what one might recognize as the sort of thing Jesus of Nazareth went around teaching. *The Gospel of Thomas* is fascinating reading, but falls *theologically* short of the "canon."

What we find, therefore, is that built in to the very concept of "the Bible," there is already a theological framework. It comes from the God who created all things, called out his people Israel, delivered them from slavery and into a land of promise, gave them prophets, priests and kings, and then Jesus, whose life, teachings, deeds, death and resurrection, were seen to be at the very heart of God's purposes, before the coming of the Holy Spirit and the beginnings of the church. When written documents came along which encouraged constructively the task of reflection on, and the living out of, this story, they were admitted into the New Testament. *This* is in fact what we were after with our pursuit of the doctrine of inspiration: a way of understanding scripture as useful for the tasks of Christian living. Yes, this is a circular process, of texts and traditions feeding into each other, but it is inevitably circular, and not viciously so (perhaps again it is a spiraling process).

It is a process hidden away in the name "New Testament" itself, which comes from the Latin phrase for "new covenant."[12] This phrase has the basic ambiguity as to whether it means that these scriptures *are* the new testament/covenant, or whether they are *about* the new testament/covenant. Either way this observation brings us back to a view of inspired New Testament scripture which sees it as providing us with access to the central story of Jesus and all he did and accomplished, understood according to the rule of faith, or the "measure" of faith with which God has measured out understanding to us.

---

12. For New Testament uses of the phrase see 1 Cor 11:25; 2 Cor 3:6; Luke 22:20 (though compare Matt 26:28; Mark 14:24). Note also 2 Cor 3:14, Gal 4:24; Eph 2:12.

8

The Authority of Scripture

Learning to Live with the Bible

I WAS SITTING IN a panel discussion on biblical interpretation, which is not something I do often, but which had happened as a response to an interesting sermon on the book of Nehemiah. The sermon had argued that much of the book of Nehemiah, which concerns the rebuilding of Jerusalem after the exile, does not apply today. In particular, we are not expecting the rebuilding of the temple in modern-day Jerusalem: these kinds of issues have been taken up by the way that Christ in the New Testament fulfills all these various hopes and expectations of the Jewish people.

The panel discussion was throwing backwards and forwards the question of whether the book of Nehemiah applies or not, and then which bits of it apply, and why and when, and I was there because I was supposed to know something about hermeneutics, even if I was not particularly knowledgeable about the book of Nehemiah. I had not managed to say anything helpful, at least as far as I could see, and I was getting more and more confused by the various arguments about whether this or that bit of scripture applied to us, when suddenly an idea struck me: the problem was not in the issue of what the book of Nehemiah was about, but the problem was with what we meant by the world "applied." I opened my mouth: "I don't think the Bible applies at all," I began, but I did not get much further, because this idea was perceived by all concerned as so far off the map as not to be worth taking seriously. But I have become convinced that the idea is worth taking seriously, and so although I would no longer put the point in quite the same way, in this chapter I will basically defend the view that we are usually muddled when we talk about "applying the Bible," and that there are better ways of saying what such language is trying to say.

Perhaps something similar can be said about notions of biblical authority too. Indeed authority and "application" seem to be two sides of the same coin. In the end, the Bible is not fundamentally about principles to be applied, or about authoritative rules to be obeyed. The book of Nehemiah, in any case, is thin on principles and rules, which is why it is a particularly bad candidate for "applying to us," although I have seen various attempts to turn the book into a repository of insights on (Christian) leadership, which has always seemed a bit of a stretch. Nehemiah is a story, and in a different sort of way, so is the whole Bible. To live with the Bible is to live with a story. This chapter, then, is a consideration of what that means for the questions of biblical authority and "applying the Bible."

The phrases "biblical authority" or "authority of the Bible" are so familiar that we tend not to think much about what they could possibly mean. More commonly, people just assume they know what such labels are talking about and then jump into debating whether or not the Bible has such authority or not. On some matters, the debate does not always seem a lot more sophisticated than "yes it does"/"no it doesn't." But the very fact that biblical authority is itself the topic of discussion may not be a good sign. As Nicholas Lash put it, "Authority is rarely, if ever, claimed or asserted until it is on the way to being lost."[1] What kind of authority would we want to say that the Bible has? Perhaps it has moral or ethical authority. To say that the Bible has this kind of authority would suggest that in moral and ethical matters, what the Bible says is right. No carrying objects around on the Sabbath, then.

Interestingly, many people who take this line end up with the kind of morality that reflects quite well on their own way of living. The Bible turns out to be in favor of an honest hard day's work for those putting in the honest hard days, but it is in favor of the poor if you ask the poor what it is about. Whether the Bible really has one consistent moral opinion about smoking, or drinking, or dancing, or swearing, or tax returns, or fair trade coffee, or any of the other key social issues in the rural and small-town world of two or three thousand years ago is another matter.

---

1. Lash, *Seeing in the Dark*, 86.

(It is not even obvious as to whether the Bible has a consistent opinion on lying, for that matter.)

Perhaps we could make progress by suggesting that the Bible's authority is "religious" or "theological." In other words, what it says about how to live the religious life, or what it says about God, is authoritative, even when all those sayings are couched in strange and far-off cultural ways. But there are problems here too. This kind of approach works well if one keeps one's distance from the text. I tend to think that one ends up with the God of introductory school classes in Religious Education. My very first Religious Education lesson at school left a strong impression. We had to memorize the meanings of three words about God: "omniscient," "omnipresent," and "eternal." It was only many years later that it occurred to me that the first two of these words do not feature much in the Bible. (We also had to memorize Isaiah 55:8–9, and I do not know which version this was, but I memorized, "My thoughts, says the Lord, are not like yours, and my ways are different from yours, for as high as the heavens are above the earth so high are my ways and thoughts above yours," and this is close to the NRSV when I look it up, although I memorized it more as one long polysyllabic word: "mythoughtssaysthelordarenotlikeyoursand . . ." Interestingly enough, we might note that this is closer to the way the ancient manuscripts of the Bible were written, as we saw in chapter 1. I rather think that Isaiah 55:8–9 was chosen to cover our teacher in case we ever felt that Religious Education lessons made no sense.)

It can be a matter of some disbelief to people such as myself, brought up with this kind of philosopher's god, actually to read the Bible and find that it talks of a God who "repents." It does this in the flood story (Genesis 6:6–7), in the wonderful book of Jonah (Jonah 3:10), and in 1 Samuel 15:11, where the word of the Lord comes to Samuel and says, "I regret that I made Saul king." Samuel obviously had the same Religious Education teacher as I did, because he cannot quite believe it either, and takes the first chance he has to harangue King Saul by saying, "The Lord has torn the kingdom of Israel from you this very day, and . . . will not recant or change his mind; for he is not a mortal, that he should change his mind" (15:28–29). This is another example where paying close attention to the text of the Bible is a quick way of dispensing with theories about what the Bible must surely say.[2]

2. Although it is not really our topic, let us clarify just a little. The word (*nacham*

Returning to our main topic, we could add other kinds of authority to our list of ways in which the Bible might be thought to be authoritative. Some say the Bible has "salvific" (or "soteriological") authority: in other words it is authoritative on the matter of "how to be saved." This tends to lead to the small number of verses that directly address this topic assuming a remarkable importance. Others, mainly in more recent times, insist that it must have factual authority: a status as a dispenser of scientific truths that leaves it tangled up in arguments about such topics as six-day creation, dinosaurs, the sun standing still, evolution, and who Adam and Eve's children married. This should really be enough to warn off anyone from going down this fossil-strewn path. Perhaps the Bible has authority about matters of philosophy or general knowledge, such as what truth is; or a kind of authority on matters psychological, correctly dividing the human self into its three constituent parts of spirit, soul, and body in 1 Thessalonians 5:23. This seems no more assured than that the bowels are the location of compassion, as the Hebrew idiom has it frequently throughout the Old Testament. Thus Jeremiah 31:20: "My heart yearns for him; I have great compassion," according to the NIV, though Hebrew readers are regaled with the divine observation: "my bowels rumble." This sort of biblical language must simply be understood to reflect the idioms and conventions of its day. When scripture has God being "slow to anger" in one of its most famous and oft-repeated characterizations (fundamentally in Exodus 34:6), the Hebrew is "long of nostrils." The logic may be clear to students of dragon mythology (long nostrils = slow to anger; short nostrils = quick to anger), but we do not in practice have any difficulty recognizing that this is language that has to be interpreted appropriately before we could begin to have a meaningful discussion about biblical authority.

What this survey of unlikely ways of pinning down biblical authority shows us is that we really need to backtrack and ask a more fundamental question in the first place: Why do we want to talk about biblical authority at all?

---

in Hebrew) in Genesis 6; 1 Samuel 15, and Jonah 3 can accurately be understood as a verb meaning "to change one's mind." In the KJV this was translated as "repent" on the grounds that this is a basic meaning of "repent," but the problem for readers today is the moral connotation that to repent is to turn from sin. This is not in view with instances of divine "repentance," hence the NRSV offers translations such as "regret," as we saw above. The further question of what it means for God to change his mind is beyond us here.

There have tended to be two main types of answer to this question. The first focuses on what the Bible is: its *nature*. It is, say defenders of this approach, true. It is inspired—although this is often left hanging as a rather vague point rather than being given the kind of substance we looked at in the last couple of chapters. And it is the Word of God. These are facts about it and they are such powerful facts that they simply do result in it being authoritative.

A second approach looks at what the Bible does: its *function*, and hence it is sometimes called—perhaps a bit dismissively—"functionalist." What does the Bible do? It reveals God to us, it inspires us, it transforms us. These things could be done in a whole variety of ways: a beautiful sunset might inspire us, and might even reveal God to us in some way. The *Gospel of Thomas* might reveal God to us, to recall our discussion in the previous chapter. Defenders of the first view tend to see this second view as a little too subjective. Defenders of the second view tend to think that the first view is too obsessed with stating facts, and ignores all the ways in which language achieves its effects. Each side has a good go at showing why the other is inadequate: How can the truth and inspiration of the Bible suffice if we do not pay attention to how to interpret it and the effect it has on us? How can the Bible reveal God to us in reliable ways if it is not inspired, true, and so on?

Attempts to break through this argument try a couple of different approaches to the question of authority. The first is to say that both these views offer important partial insights. We need both precisely because the *function* of the Bible is intimately tied up with its *nature*, and you cannot have one without the other. What the Bible is in itself is not really the issue. We are not concerned with the Bible when it sits on the shelf, or when it is not read. It is only once it is taken up and read and inter-preted that we can have a significant discussion about it. But then what the Bible achieves once it is read does depend on what the Bible is. To take an example, the promises of the Bible can be effective only if certain things are true about them. If the end of Matthew's Gospel sees Jesus promise that he will always be with his disciples, then it is one thing to see this as an encouragement or—loosely—an inspiration, but for it to work as a promise it has to be true that the one saying this is really Jesus, who is capable of being present in this way, in some "real" sense. Likewise, it is because the Bible is "breathed out" by God that what it says about God can be revelatory. This is what makes it more than just

Paul's or Isaiah's impressions. In other words, the function of the biblical text does depend on some true things about it. This approach falls under the heading of the study of "speech acts," which is an approach to language which points out that words achieve effects depending on who says them and in what context. On the whole it is a helpful way forward for thinking about how the nature and function of the Bible are linked.[3]

A second way ahead which has gained ground in recent years is the view that "authority" is one useful image for talking about the Bible, but it is not the only one. There are in fact many images we could use of the Bible to suggest ways in which it still speaks today, and "authoritatively" is one of them, but only one. Sometimes this argument is used more or less to reject the notion of "authority." Thus David Clines offers the intriguing possibility that the language of authority derives from male-dominated ways of thinking about how to influence and be heard:

> Strange in a way that feminists have not yet seen that "authority" is a concept from the male world of power-relations, and that a more inclusive human language of influence, encouragement and inspiration would be more acceptable to everyone and more likely to win the assent of minds as well as hearts.[4]

He does not mean "inspiration" here in the sense of "inspired scripture," but in the general sense of seeing how the Bible inspires us. This view tends towards being a little weak on specifics, but it does have the merit of taking seriously the complexity of hermeneutical thinking which clouds the way from the text to the reader. How does the book of Nehemiah inspire or influence us? This is a good question that in principle is answerable, rather unlike the problematic, "How does Nehemiah apply to us?" The difficulty with the kind of position that rules out "authority" language, though, is that something is lost which was traditionally valued. The problem is when the text is difficult, or presents us with something that we might rather not hear, "authority" language can be useful for forcing us to work at understanding it rather longer than we might if we were just waiting to discern "influence" or "encouragement." Nicholas Lash again: "There is, in our culture, a deep-laid and most unbiblical assumption that God's Word is spoken for comfort rather than

---

3. See chapter 10 below. The above argument about authority and function is developed in detail by Thiselton, "Authority and Hermeneutics."

4. Clines, *What Does Eve Do to Help?*, 48.

for truth."[5] It is not that scripture never wishes to encourage us. But if we decide ahead of time that we will screen out the uncomfortable bits, we will change the shape of our Bible reading in ways that will ultimately simply get the Bible to echo back to us what we already believed anyway.

The question of what other images could be used to describe how the Bible speaks today leads us directly into the question of "application." If the Bible were simply a historical document, of antiquarian interest only, it is doubtful that we would be overly troubled by its frequently odd details and assumptions, of the kind that we have been examining throughout this discussion. But the biblical text still speaks today for as long as people listen to it, and indeed it even speaks in odd ways when people do not really listen to it but just happen across it out of context and poorly understand it. In extreme cases it even has a kind of influence when it is attributed with saying things it simply never says. I recall a church friend once who kept his house clean because, he was sure, the Bible said that cleanliness was next to godliness.

Walter Brueggemann offers the delightful image—not intended irreverently, he assures us—of the Bible as a "compost pile": a place where new texts, once written down, are thrown on to the pile of the old ones, and as they bed down and take up residence in the canon so they grow and mutate in an unpredictable fashion to create whole new ways of looking at things.[6] The Bible as compost pile is a particularly striking offbeat metaphor for the concept of the living word today. However, in principle, it is still part of the broader discussion of the nature of biblical authority. Another—rather more common—way in which people pursue this issue is to say something more like, "The Bible applies to us today." But what does *that* mean?

The language of "applying" the Bible basically seeks somehow to bridge the gap between the Bible and us as readers. The question is: How? Does it ask, "What biblical principles arise out of the passage?" This I think is a very common way of thinking, and it has one very serious drawback. It assumes that whatever the kind of text we have, what we are *really* looking for is principles, and if we do not see them in the text then we need to find them by supplying them in order to make some sense of the text. The kind of principles involved are then typically the moral and ethical ones we considered earlier. For some biblical texts this

---

5. Lash, *Seeing in the Dark*, 94.

6. Brueggemann, *Texts Under Negotiation*, 61–62.

can work. In general, however, it results in forcing all biblical texts into this moral and ethical framework.

We can try to simplify the question and ask, "What does the Bible say today?" One well-known series of devotional commentaries bears just such a title: "The Bible Speaks Today." This is fair enough, but in itself does not constitute an answer to *how* it speaks today. On a personal level, many Bible readers want to ask, "What does the Bible say on a personal and immediately relevant level to me?" Again this leaves us guessing about how we can evaluate different "applications" of the Bible. A friend of mine used to enjoy appealing to the story of Samson in the book of Judges whenever the conversation turned to the vexed matter of God's "guidance" in daily life. Samson sees a Philistine woman at Timnah in Judges 14:1 and after his parents try hard to dissuade him from marrying outside of his own people, he resolves the discussion with the forthright appeal, "Get her for me, because she pleases me" (v. 3). His father and mother, says the story as it continues on its untroubled way, "did not know that this was from the Lord" (v. 4). Here, my friend would say, was one of God's more unusual means of guidance: holy lust.

A more promising way ahead—and there have been hints of it through not just this chapter but the whole second part of this book— is to say that the question of application is best understood as saying, "What does a biblical passage *reveal* to me about . . . ?" Of course, immediately one must specify what it is that we are asking about. Perhaps it is God, or Christ, or creation. The key point here is that the Bible says much about many things, many more in fact than it ever intended to discuss, and that does mean that a lot more is pulled into the "biblical" orbit than anyone ever intended. But in line with our discussion in the previous chapter about the rule of faith, perhaps we can propose that what the Bible does specifically—and in particular what it does that sets it apart from other literature—is that it *reveals* God to us. What we have arrived at is the argument that we need a doctrine of revelation in order to read the Bible wisely.

What then does the Bible reveal? Of course some might say that it reveals a lot of facts or truths. However, we recall what we said above about how language is engaged in many activities other than just stating facts, and also we recall that the biblical canon was built around something other than being a collection of facts—in other words such a claim underestimates the force of the argument about "the rule of faith." The in-built theological standard we saw at work in our canon discussion suggested the revelation of the Bible centers around God, through both testaments, and in particular Jesus—his life and death, his teaching and deeds, and most of all his resurrection—in the New Testament. Without that central God-focus, the whole of Christianity can become a great program for moral living and looking after our neighbors, but it lacks the essential ingredient that makes it Christianity. Recall the argument in chapter 1 that we must read the scriptures in the light of Jesus and understand Jesus in the light of the scriptures. There I allowed this way of putting the matter needed to be broadened to take in the doctrine of the Trinity rather than just saying that it is "all about Jesus." Here too we need to take the broader view. As theologians would say at this point, the Bible is God's Trinitarian self-revelation. In fact, this is exactly what Karl Barth said in his powerful article on "The Strange New World within the Bible."[7] We read this extraordinary story of Abraham, of Moses, of the prophets, of Jesus, of the early church, and what do we make of it? Is it an account of history? Yes, in a way, but such an odd and selective one that this cannot have been the point. Is it a book of morality? "Large parts of the Bible," says Barth, "are almost useless to the school in its moral curriculum,"[8] a point not lost on any good moral parent who has read the Bible to their children and stumbled over the stories of death to Sabbath wood-carriers, incest and rape in and out of Israel, or the matter of "holy lust" considered above. Barth is equally unhappy with the notion that we find "religion" in the Bible—at least if we define religion as the ways in which people organize their lives and thoughts in pursuit of God. No, what we find in the Bible is God reaching down to God's people everywhere, throughout history and onward to the present day: the revelation of God, who is Father, Son, and Holy Spirit. More specifically, we find the story is told in order for God to reveal that this is his particular Trinitarian identity.

Barth's argument has not really been bettered. The emphasis on the Bible as God's *story* has become very prominent in recent years. This is partly because it appeals to the more story-oriented leanings of what some people call our "postmodern" world. But it is partly because it really does seem to do more justice to the nature of the Bible to describe it

---

7. Barth, "Strange New World."

8. Ibid., 38.

as a story than as a work of doctrine or even—narrowly understood—as "systematic theology."

N. T. Wright invites us to imagine scripture along the lines of a five-act Shakespeare play. In this image, the biblical text takes us through the first few acts, leaving us, as the church today, to improvise the final act while remaining "in character."[9] We work within the possibilities of those first acts: creation, fall, Israel, Christ, the church. This is our story, as God's people, and we "implement" it today. Not only is this a creative and persuasive account of biblical authority, as it sets out to be, but it actually offers a very good answer to the question of what it means to "apply the Bible" today. It gets us away from the constant problem in the contemporary church of reducing the Bible to the level of morality by finding everywhere within it moral principles for us to apply, as if the gospel were the good news that we all get to try harder than ever to be good moral people. Wright's model perhaps suggests that our task is more to learn how to act "in character" than how to apply specific moral principles, though of course these two ways of looking at it are not unrelated. Even more it suggests that we are to be focused on the God at the center of the biblical story. The language of Moule may reflect a way of putting the point which dates it slightly, but the theology is just right: "The Bible is not itself so much a compass or a chart, as directions for finding the Pilot; and he it is who will be to us both compass and chart and will steer us through."[10] In fact, one could also say that Shakespeare's five-act plays are not exactly common currency these days either. Let me close this chapter, then, with an attempt to sketch out this whole approach to scripture's authority and application with an example drawn from more recent times.

I will never forget the dramatic experience of watching the first *Star Wars* film when it first came out in the cinemas in the late 1970s. As an impressionable young boy in the pre-video and pre-computer age, the film completely caught my imagination. In particular, the spectacular concluding scene of the Rebel X-wing attack on the Death Star included a shot of the entry of the small spaceships swinging down into the Death Star trenches for their final approach. I sat glued to my seat as the picture on the enormous screen in the cinema lurched one way and then the other to simulate the twisting flight down into the depths. In fact it was

9. Wright, *Scripture*, 89–93. See further his "How Can the Bible Be Authoritative?"

10. Moule, *Forgiveness and Reconciliation*, 223.

a cinematic breakthrough in itself: the first time that moving camera shots could be computer controlled to achieve this sense of motion and involvement. You could feel the reality of the moment, as real as any car ride, plane flight, or bike ride down a dark alley. To emerge, blinking, into the sunlight of a quiet suburb a few minutes later was to leave the world of *Star Wars* and re-enter my normal world, but as a changed person. I was now someone who had survived a flight to the Death Star and back.

On the whole I am delighted with the advance in technology that now allows me to watch this self-same film on disc on the tiny TV screen we have in our living room. But the moment of approach to the Death Star is never the same, for there in the small corner of the room—surrounded by bookshelves, pictures, toys, phone calls, the noise of cars outside and footballs flying over the fence—the twisting camera work does not make me lurch in my seat at all. It is all too small-scale, and does not overcome my world. Neither can I fully enter its world.

Apart from the obvious "application" that I should buy a bigger television, what is the point? I recall preaching on Acts 16:16–34, the story of Paul and Silas in prison in Philippi. Since I had studied the passage through that week, I arrived on Sunday morning quite impressed by it. But the rest of the congregation arrived on Sunday morning not having the faintest idea that this would be the set passage. Instead they were still fairly preoccupied with other things, the typical ups and downs of any week of living in our complicated and tiring world. The passage was read, as scripture is always read as part of the service, and then I walked up to preach. I realized, as I listened to the reading and looked around the church, that for almost everyone, this passage was playing on a small screen television. It was probably a television in the kitchen, and they had one eye on not burning the lunch, and one eye on the story of Acts 16. There goes the slave girl, there go her owners, there go Paul and Silas into prison, there they are singing hymns, and then—look at that!—there's an earthquake. They get out, the jailer believes, everyone gets baptized, and then it is time to put the potatoes on and check the dessert.

This small-screen viewing of the story is, I think, typical of the way most Christians are exposed to scripture most of the time. It leaves the average reader—or hearer—of scripture pondering just what sort of "application" one could make from this Acts 16 passage. I duly informed the congregation that if ever they were in prison in first-century Philippi for exorcising the demon of a slave girl, and there was an earthquake during a time of midnight hymn singing, then this passage would apply perfectly to them and show them exactly what to do. This met with some surprise, of course, but it did lead on to an interesting sermon. In fact, I tried then to suggest that the only way to hear a word from God from this passage was to stop playing it on our kitchen-corner television set, and watch it on the big screen of the cinema, gripped by the earthquake just as I had once been by *Star Wars*. Watch it this way and then when you emerge blinking from church half an hour later, you might be changed by what you have seen. In this case, you might be changed by the extraordinary God who was at work in that passage: a God who will pin you to your seat if you stop and watch, but whose hand you might not even notice on the mini-TV version.

The "application" of the story comes through the wholesale effect of being transformed by watching/hearing it properly, as a word about who this God is. To meet with God in the story is to be changed. There is no guarantee that God will shake the foundations of any prison you might ever end up in, and I knew that this would be a false word of hope to bring from a passage such as this. But there is a guarantee that the God who is revealed in this passage is the same one the congregation lives with today. That guarantee comes from accepting that this scripture is "inspired," built to match the "rule of faith," and thus authoritative in this strange new way that we have been considering in this chapter.

If this is what we mean by saying that the Bible "applies" to us then all well and good. On the whole I tend to think that it is not what most people mean, and so there may be some merit in saying that the Bible does not "apply." But either way, if it engages people, and helps them take God more seriously, then that is what matters.

PART THREE

Hermeneutical Perspectives

9

Revelation

Unveiled Eyes and Unveiled Text

THE BOOK OF REVELATION is the place where it all comes together—theologically, historically, literarily, imaginatively, and hermeneutically. This chapter offers a way in to reading Revelation that tries to bring together the various insights of earlier chapters. To many this may sound like trying to explain the difficult by appealing to the impossible.

Revelation is too often the happy hunting ground of religious lunatics and extremists, or of people whose great concern in life appears to be trying to work out when the "rapture" will happen or how "premillennial" you are. For most of the rest of us, it is a hunting ground that is closed to the public for the foreseeable future, awaiting development at the end of the world, and veiled from our understanding. But this is to miss out on one of the most remarkable and—though this is often thought hard to believe—one of the most immediately relevant books of the entire Bible. In particular, we concluded the last chapter by saying that the Bible is fundamentally about God's self-revelation. In the book of Revelation the veil, which so often hides God from our eyes is drawn back. And what do we see when that happens? If we play it out on the cinema-sized screen, rather than the kitchen TV, I think we see something like this.

We see John, on the island of Patmos (1:9). We are, then, looking at a historical text. We might want to know that Patmos is a Greek island, and that John might be in prison, perhaps because he was publicly testifying to Jesus. The only thing most people do know about the book is that he is going to write seven letters to the different churches in the region, which will get us as far as the end of chapter 3. Then a door will open in heaven, there will be lots of choruses and hymns—worship of the lamb on the throne—and then·after that it will all gradually become weird, wild, and either worrisome or wonderful, depending on where we stand.

The letters to the seven churches, which are really several sections of one letter sent to all seven churches, such that each one gets to hear what is good and bad about all the others, is usually the only section of the book preached or studied in many churches today. We will therefore be brief with the seven letters, except to note that the reason why there are seven of them is because seven was a number of completeness in the early church, and thus in the Bible, and it recurs frequently through the book. We may also note that the function of these seven letters seems to be that these seven churches represent, in some sense, the whole church. Some are good and some are in a mess, and each faces different trials and possible blessings. We can almost always relate our own position to one of them, and so we are reminded that the book of Revelation will speak to our kind of situation too.

This chapter is not intended as a short "commentary" on Revelation, but we do want to see how an awareness of different contexts for the book can help our reading. First, what sort of literature is it? It is known as "apocalyptic." This word, which we have come across once or twice already, has increasingly come into popular usage through the medium of films such as *Apocalypse Now*, with its dramatic images of the military helicopter assault on an unsuspecting Vietcong village against the soundtrack of Wagner's "Ride of the Valkyries" one of the most unforgettable sequences in modern cinema, in its own wide screen and appalling way. That kind of "apocalyptic" imagery is what many people see in the book of Revelation too, and in one notorious case the locusts from the bottomless pit in 9:7–11, which are described as having wings like the noise of many battle chariots, and tails that sting like scorpions, have been described as prophecies of modern-day helicopters. We shall see shortly that this is a hopelessly over-literal way of approaching a text such as this.

In fact "apocalypse" is simply the Greek word for "revelation," and both these words basically mean "unveiling." Apocalyptic literature was not uncommon at the time of the book of Revelation, although this is the only book-length version of it in the New Testament. The most important thing to understand about it, in terms of its theology and its historical classification as apocalyptic literature, is that apocalyptic is *not about the end of the world*. At least, not in the sense that one might think. What it is actually about is *revealing*, or *unveiling*. In this case what it reveals is God—the God of Jesus Christ, and of the Holy Spirit, who is the Lord even over the chaotic world of the end of the first century, where John has been thrown in prison and all seems lost for a church facing the Roman Empire.[1] When God is revealed as he is in the book of Revelation, something does end, but it is not the world. It is the way one sees the world. This unveiling changes our whole outlook on the world; we begin to see the world around us in ways we had not seen it before. We should say then that Revelation is a book about *the end of the world as we know it*, in the sense that it changes the way we know—and changes what we know—about this world in which we live.

The unveiling begins at the point where many readers and churches leave the book, at the beginning of chapter 4: "After this I looked, and there in heaven a door stood open!" (4:1) How many doors are there in heaven and how far do we have to look to see them, or see past them? In a famous passage in John 14, Jesus said that in his Father's house there were "many mansions" (John 14:2).[2] Perhaps there are enough doors for everyone to have their own room . . . ? Clearly this is not the way to take such language. The opening door in heaven symbolizes the revealing to John of this God-centered reality in heaven.

What does John see? How he wrote it all down we shall never know, although the careful literary structure and repeated patterns of the book suggest that he took some time to translate the stunning vision that follows into the literary text which tells us about it. But the key thing that he sees is Jesus, seated on the throne. Jesus is a lamb (5:6), even though

1. We need not discuss here the tricky question of whether the Roman Empire was engaged in actual persecution of the church in AD 95–96, the traditional date of the book. It was often argued that the church in Revelation was facing actual persecution, but the persuasive thesis of Thompson, *Book of Revelation*, is that the book seeks to provoke its readers into seeing the threats of the day, rather than reflecting the experience of persecution (for which we have no independent evidence).

2. Or "dwelling places," as modern translations such as the NRSV put it. This is doubtless because of the oddity of having mansions in a house . . . an image that relies on the ancient idea of a "house" as an extended network of dwellings for all the different "nuclear families" to live together. As we have come to assume that each family has its own separate house, so we have lost the extended-family sense of John 14:2.

he has just been described as the Lion of Judah (5:5), which is a significant contrast between an image of power and strength, and an image of
sacrifice and suffering represented by the cross. What is the lamb holding? He is holding a scroll (5:1) and nobody can open it. This scroll may
be one key to the whole book.[3]

There is a very simple reason why no one can open the scroll: it
is sealed. No one is worthy to open the seals, of which there are seven,
which should not surprise us. The scroll is what will contain *the* revelation of the book of Revelation, and so one good question to ask is how it
is opened and when. As we scroll down quickly through chapters 6–10
we discover that the opening of the seals is a significant activity, and
that out of the first four of them come the infamous "four horsemen of
the apocalypse" (6:1–8). Each seal clearly seems to be standing for some
event or observation about the world we live in, or more precisely the
world in which John's first readers lived. More precisely still, they were
John's first *hearers*, since the book was designed for oral performance,
according to 1:3.[4]

The seals are interrupted after six out of seven of them are opened,
and the interruption is also a sealing—of the 144,000—who seem to
represent the people of God understood as a kind of standing army,
ready to fight the forces of evil.[5] The point here, however, is simply this:
the scroll is still not opened, because the seventh seal is not opened
until 8:1. As soon as it is opened there is a sequence of seven trumpets being blown by the angels. These angels are from the throne room
scene back in chapters 4–5, and so we are still watching the scroll being unrolled at this point. The trumpets, like the seals, symbolize the
terrible events going on upon the earth, and they take us up to the
appearance of "another mighty angel" in 10:1. What does this angel

---

3. I follow here the argument of Bauckham, *Climax of Prophecy*, 243–57. This
work and Bauckham's shorter book, *Theology*, have shaped the approach to the book
of Revelation taken in the present chapter. It is of course true that there are many other
lines of interpretation possible, but in my judgment this one is persuasive.

4. One wonders if this verse still offers a blessing today to anyone who reads the
book aloud?

5. This might explain the striking verse at 14:4 about the fact that the 144,000 "have
not defiled themselves with women," since those preparing for combat were not to engage in sexual activity—a view developed from considering Leviticus 15:16 alongside
passages which required holiness of warriors.

have in its hand? A little scroll, not sealed, but open. Then in 10:6 the angel says, "there will be no more delay."

It is helpful to recognize that the entire story up to this point has been the preparation for the revelation, which is going to be found in the contents of the scroll. Now John receives the scroll from the angel's hand, and in 10:9 is told to eat it, which he then does. Here we have the "seer—the author of this apocalyptic book—eating the scroll that contains the message to be unveiled. In verse 11 he is then told, "You must prophesy again about many people and nations and languages and kings." The idea of eating a scroll from God is found in Ezekiel 2:8—3:11. The book of Ezekiel is probably one of the few candidates for being even more obscure than Revelation, but in this short section the point is clear: Ezekiel eats the scroll and thus "inwardly digests" (somewhat literally) the message which God wants him to proclaim. So too here with John in Revelation. For Ezekiel the scroll was as sweet as honey, as it was for John, but in John's case it left a nasty aftertaste. John's message will be one of bitter judgment as much as of hope.

Thus we arrive at chapter 11 as the long-awaited contents of the scroll. What may immediately strike the reader of Revelation here is that as soon as chapter 11 begins we find ourselves completely lost in the midst of some very obscure and unexplained symbolism. Odd though the book may have been to this point—and we have indeed skipped over many points of detail and explanation—it has been possible to follow the developing plot of the build-up to the opening of the scroll. But now in chapter 11 everything changes. This is perhaps a further indication that it is only now that we have reached the actual "revelation." Before proceeding to it, it is only fair to acknowledge that there are of course many different interpretations of Revelation, and not all of them see these two scrolls in chapters 5 and 10 as the same. The second one is indeed called a "little scroll" whereas the first one is just a scroll. But with Revelation, it is the clarity of the big picture that counts in interpretation, and the difficulty of all the details needs to be measured against the overall understanding of the story. In this particular case it does not make such a big difference whether the two scrolls are one and the same. But it does matter that "the revelation" itself only begins in chapter 11, which allows us to see the first half of the book as a kind of preparation for its main message.

The reader will have to look elsewhere for help with the many details beyond chapter 11.[6] However, in many ways chapter 11 itself is the key, since it seems to be a kind of summary of the contents of the scroll, which is repeated and developed in subsequent chapters. In any case, chapter 11 is so full of strange details that it will keep us busy enough. The risk is that we will lose the overall focus if we get lost in the details.

To take one example: What are we to make of the 42 months and the 1260 days in 11:2–3? A little bit of elementary mathematics will tell us that these are basically the three and a half years which famously concerned Daniel (in Daniel 7:25 and 12:7). It might take us that long to read all the different theories about what this means. It is enough to know, however, that it is essentially a way of referring to a time of great persecution, apparently described in months from the point of view of evil, but in days from the point of view of the two faithful "witnesses." We could recall that Daniel too was written at a time when God's people were in confusion and disarray, unsure how to relate to the world powers under which they lived. Revelation often draws on details of Old Testament symbolism in this way. Likewise the olive trees and the lamp stands in 11:4 will remind the attentive reader of Zechariah, albeit that not so many readers today would be alert to the reference. Lamp stands, however, featured in Revelation 1:20, where they were interpreted for us: a lamp stand is a church. This is perhaps to point to the nature of a church as a source of light for the surrounding people. Again, while the specifics may be obscure, the big picture can still be grasped. We will aim for this as we read Revelation 11.

The two witnesses in 11:3, who play a key role in the chapter, are two in number because in the Old Testament you needed two witnesses to have a testimony that was considered valid.[7] Chapter 11 describes these two witnesses in terms deliberately reminiscent of Moses and Elijah, turning the water to blood as Moses did in the plagues in Egypt in the book of Exodus, and shutting up the skies so there was no rain, as Elijah did in the book of Kings. We last saw Moses and Elijah on the Mount of Transfiguration, where Jesus was preparing for his *exodos* ("departure") in Jerusalem. Revelation is perhaps picking up on the same story as the Gospels. But we should also note that the two are not actually named

6. In addition to Bauckham's two books, already noted, a most useful (and not excessively detailed) commentary on Revelation is Rowland, *Revelation*.

7. See Deuteronomy 17:6 and 19:15.

here. This is probably because these two witnesses are not simply Moses and Elijah, but rather they are also the whole church, seen together as faithful witnesses to Jesus.

Is this faithful witness successful? The overall message of the book is "Yes!" And yet this chapter first tells us: "No!" And then "Yes!" Yes and no. How does this work? Is the church to be successful in its witness to Jesus? If we can answer this question then we might begin to see what the book of Revelation is trying to show us, or *reveal* to us.

In 11:7 the beast kills the witnesses and they are left dead in the street. We do not yet know this beast—we have not been introduced, as it were—but when we are introduced, in chapter 13, we will not forget it quickly. Where is this street? Verse 8 identifies its location, but does so, as it says in the text, "spiritually" (*pneumatikōs*). The location is Sodom. Or is it Egypt—the land of slavery before the Exodus? Or is it in fact Jerusalem, "where also their Lord was crucified"? Does John not know? Not at all: he is saying that the church's witness seems to fall—to fail—in any place where evil seems to win, and as his list of cities suggests, this seems to happen a lot. New York. London. Mumbai. Berlin. Mexico City. Wherever humankind gathers itself together to create cities, from the great city of Babel on through Babylon, Rome and up until today, one result seems to be that God gets pushed out to the margins of the city, and of human life.

One way of understanding the city in the Bible is as humanity "writ large," notoriously self-sufficient, and turned away from its creator God. The idea seems to be that people are inclined to turn away from any need for a creator God when everyone can see that the city is a creation of the humans who live there. In one of the most significant of such narratives, the story of the tower of Babel in Genesis 11:1–9, we read of a tower that reaches up to the heavens, suggesting that everything humankind has achieved it did itself, with good planning, clever resource management, exploitation of the planet's non-renewable resources, and the discreet deployment of cheap labor bused in from the outskirts, or from the farthest reaches of empire, wherever that may be.

What do we see when we look at the city? We see the failure of the church's witness, mirroring the failure of its Lord, who after throwing himself at Jerusalem, all those years and centuries ago, was left to hang on a cross and die. He was not even offered the dignity of a private death away from evil eyes. In 11:9, this death is even shamefully left on the streets, and in verse 10 the "the inhabitants of the earth" rub it in our faces, celebrating and exchanging presents. What might they be saying to themselves? Let's build the biggest celebration of them all. Let's call it Christmas, then turn it into an event that celebrates the success of our self-sufficient economies, and then let's disallow "religious" elements for fear of offending anybody. Let's exchange the costliest presents we can find, perhaps some fashionable trainers, made by a thirteen-year-old girl in a sweat-shop in a shanty town in the far East who is paid not enough to feed herself or allow any in her family to escape from the relentless cycle of poverty and depression.

Much of the time, that seems to be what the world we live in looks like: a world where Christian faith seems entirely deluded about the idea that it has made or can or will make any difference. Is that the bottom line?

But it all changes in verse 11. The third day. Or actually three and a half days in this case, rather like "on the third day" at the tomb was really only thirty-six hours later, with the number being stretched here to match up to Daniel's "three and a half." Something is about to happen that will so affect the nature of our reality that one might think even two and two will not make four any more, but will add up to three and a half. After three and a half days, the breath (or "spirit," *pneuma*) of life whips into the dead bodies, of the two witnesses, and of the church, and raises them to their feet. This is resurrection, which again was foreshadowed in Ezekiel, when the valley of dry bones came alive. The imagery here shifts swiftly between the third day—the day of Jesus' own resurrection—and the resurrected witness of the church. Verse 12 sees the ascension to heaven. The enemies are terrified. Cue earthquakes: the shaking of the foundations of the city, any city, shaken down to its roots, as the witness to Jesus turns out, after all, to be triumphant.

Where does this resurrection life come from? This is the deeper reality that for most of us, most of the time, is veiled behind the deceptive way the world seems to be. The witness of the church to Jesus turns out to represent a deeper reality in our world. It is deeper than the marginalization of that witness in the modern world, whether it is in the city, in the press, or in the secularization and strange greed of Christmas. By the power of that breath of life, the church does make a difference.

Is that the way we see the world? Is this revelation an end to an old way of seeing the world—the end of the world as we knew it? This would seem to be the point. When the beast gets its full introduction in chapter

13 it is so clearly Rome, the empire nobody would ever have believed would pass away, and yet which is now a chapter in the history books. The whole world loved Rome: the *pax romana* was the great gift of peace that made progress and development possible. If Rome offered to run things for you, you signed up and paid taxes, and reaped the benefits. You would have had to be as stubborn as a Pharisee to say otherwise. But Revelation says: do not look at Rome that way. Think of it as a harlot, a prostitute, a whore clothed in great jewels and wondrous clothes, but actually the foulest and worst of them all (17:1–6). Rome is captured as a kind of Babylon—standing for everything that opposed God's people. But Rome in the book of Revelation thus serves as a kind of symbol, which we can discern in various other "empires" down through history. Perhaps the key is always whether such an "empire," whatever the benefits it might bestow upon its citizens, truly honors the God of Jesus Christ in its conduct. Such a question will inevitably ask how it treats its weakest and most marginalized members. By these (prophetic) standards, how do our civilizations measure up? Are they awaiting unveiling, guilty of all that is said of Rome in the extraordinary lament of Revelation 18: the fall of Babylon, or rather the collapse of the Empire, wherever and whenever that happens?

In the book of Revelation, the veil that separates God's way of seeing reality from our own usual ways of seeing is drawn back. The door in heaven is opened (4:1), and then the temple in heaven is opened (11:19), and finally heaven itself is opened (19:11) and Jesus rides out victoriously on the white horse. This triumphant ride is the last appearance of the "Word of God" in scripture, as living and active as ever, to borrow a description from Hebrews 4:12–13. At the end of the book of Revelation the Word of God completes in final recreating victory the creative work begun by the Word of God in Genesis 1, where everything was spoken into existence by God (which was really the point, rather than the six days).

As the rest of the book goes on to recount, the aim of all of this was that people from all nations would gather around the throne in the end. Every tribe and people and language will stand before the throne. The resurrection of Jesus becomes the resurrected witness of God's faithful people, so that in spite of the fact that everything in the world around us pushes Christianity out to the edges and suggests that it might just be a primitive superstition that we are now finally growing out of, it turns out that God is still the one in charge of world history, and of today's nations and empires. Despite all appearances to the contrary, he is still engaged in the infinitely loving process of drawing all people to himself, and of bringing everything together in Christ. These emphases are found especially in such magnificent hymnic passages of the New Testament as Ephesians 1:10 and Colossians 1:15–20. The language there may not be apocalyptic, but the extraordinary scope of the vision is the same.

It is true that we cannot remain, on a day-to-day level, in the world of the book of Revelation. However, once we have started to see it, we can no longer continue in this world as if nothing had happened. We are like the "wise men" of T. S. Eliot's poem "Journey of the Magi," who have seen the Christ child and now can never go back to the way things were: they returned to their former kingdoms "no longer at ease here, in the old dispensation"—the familiar made new by the grasping of the strange new world within the Bible.[8]

To see the world with unveiled eyes, as it is portrayed in Revelation, *should* leave us "no longer at ease here." It should draw us back constantly to scripture to keep alive a fresh vision of God, and of God's way of seeing reality.

8. See Eliot, "Journey," 104.

10

Action

Scripture as the Speech Acts of God

WE HAVE SPENT A lot of time in this book thinking about the biblical text, and then also about how we read. As we consider some hermeneutical perspectives on Bible reading in these final chapters, we may be wondering how exactly the study of scripture can be understood to transform us. What makes the difference between reading the words on the page, and becoming new people as we read? This chapter and the next explore a couple of ways in which we are transformed through the process of reading.

The notion of reading the words on a page is in some ways a relatively recent aspect of how the church reads scripture. For the vast majority of pre-Reformation believers, for example, the Word of God was encountered as a spoken voice: the preached word of the sermon. In such settings it seems to make more evident sense to describe the biblical text as living and active than it does today when the Bible is more bought than read, more repackaged than received, and more often gathering dust on the shelf than either living or active. That the words of scripture themselves could be living and active puts us in the area of "speech act theory"—a speech act being an act performed in (or by) speech. Speech act theory is one useful hermeneutical tool among many today, and we mentioned it briefly in an earlier chapter in connection with thinking about biblical authority. However, much of the time it is explained with such complexity that it remains more or less inaccessible to the average Bible reader in the process. This chapter is therefore a brief attempt to mediate to a wider audience some of the ways in which current thinking about "speech acts" seems to offer some helpful ways forward in looking at how scripture functions in the life of the reader.[1]

To refresh our thinking: hermeneutics is the science or art of interpretation, and the challenge facing Bible readers today is to hear the voice of God across the immense gap that separates our modern and/or postmodern world from the "world of the text," by which we may be referring to one of two things. Either we may have in mind the world in which the biblical text was produced (such as first-century Corinth), or we may envisage the world which unfolds before us in the biblical text, whether that be the apocalyptic drama of the book of Revelation, or the make-believe world of a parable, or the hand-held-camera documentary style of Mark's gospel. For one brief moment, at the moment of production, the worlds of text and reader are the same thing. For the rest, time marches on and the task of interpretation interposes itself between the text and ourselves. In common parlance: there is a big gap between the Bible and today.

The names of this gap are legion: history, culture, worldview, language, and, depending on one's theological perspective, theology. Across the gap lie various bridges, or, perhaps more accurately, bridges in various states of completion. These bridges, to stretch the image, can be understood as different "hermeneutics," and indeed sometimes as "biblical hermeneutics," depending on their point of departure.

What makes a good bridge? A good bridge links the reader with the text, allowing a two-way traffic of dialogue across it. In Gadamer's terms, the reading of the text invites a logic of question and answer by which the reader may be led to a satisfactory understanding—or "hearing"—of the text.[2] For some, as we have seen, the bridge is a matter of transporting ethical principles away from various unpromising narrative work-sites, a process which involves all manner of unlikely structuring and restructuring of the biblical text in order to turn the story into three points all beginning with "P." We saw too that many bridges appear to develop structural faults at the level of their basic assumption: they suppose the text to be an unproblematic string of assertions, and

---

1. A more detailed presentation of the ideas of this chapter may be found in Briggs "Speech-Act Theory" (2008).

2. Gadamer, *Truth and Method*, 362–79.

thus think the hermeneutic involved is simply one of trying to "apply" or "contextualize" these assertions into today's world.

There are many ways of trying to address this issue, but one way worth considering is to ask whether there might not be a basic mistake in thinking the text is all assertions in the first place. Here I want to argue we should adopt a different approach to understanding what makes up a text, considering it rather as a series of speech acts performed by an author or perhaps a narrator, and that involve the reader. In response, readers of the text invest themselves in it, and the resulting bridge we could call a "hermeneutic of self-involvement." To this end I will introduce speech acts and speech act theory, outline this hermeneutic, and then offer some illustrations of how it may help us to explain what is going on in biblical interpretation. A speech act hermeneutic is not the only bridge in town, but in certain cases, for particular types of text, it might be the high road from there to here.

WHAT ARE SPEECH ACTS?

The subject of speech act theory is neatly captured in the offbeat title of its first and most famous discussion: J. L. Austin's *How to Do Things with Words*.[3] Language, says Austin, is fundamentally "performative." It does things. More precisely, when we speak or write, we do things with it—performing acts such as promising, hinting, arguing, blessing, condemning, announcing, evoking, praising, praying, telling, and joking. This simple insight has far-reaching implications. Some studies of speech acts painstakingly classify literally hundreds of "performative verbs" and analyze how the speaker and hearer are related in them, according to whether the speaker is performing one of the five basic categories of speech act:

1) declaring something ("declaratives")
2) committing themselves to some course of action ("commissives")
3) directing the hearer in some way ("directives")
4) asserting something ("assertives")
5) expressing some psychological state ("expressives")[4]

3. Austin, *Words*.

4. See most simply Searle, *Expression and Meaning*, 1–29. Searle's *Speech Acts* ranks alongside Austin's work as a basic text of speech act theory.

Once we accept that language is irreducibly dynamic in this way, it is a short step to realizing that "the meaning of what a text states" is one dimension only of its significance and relevance to us today.

So far so good. Some people, however, like to suppose that such a view of language is best labeled "postmodern," and this is potentially misleading enough to require a brief clarification. On the one hand, whenever X labels Y as postmodern it often tells us more about X than Y, and there are enough definitions of postmodernism around to make it possible to either classify or declassify almost any thinker with this label. However, to my mind there is no obvious reason why Austin's view has anything to do with postmodernism. The confusion seems to rest in a misreading of his basic argument. Austin starts by proposing a difference between statements and performatives, and then explores the fact that it is impossible to draw a rigid distinction between them. His conclusion: a statement is a kind of performative too. To state something is, in other words, to do something. But, in Austin's view, a statement is still a different kind of act from, say, a promise or an exclamation. Those keen to find some kind of performative payoff from speech act theory rush to suggest that Austin has reduced stating a fact to the act of trying to convince somebody. Truth becomes rhetoric, and all prose turns out to be persuasion. It is no use denying that one can take this path with speech act theory: it has been taken, and indeed has sometimes seemed to be its noisiest development.[5] But it would be a great pity to let it obscure other hermeneutical options.

Austin did not live to develop anything like a full theory of speech acts, but many others have developed what he started.[6] Thus one may distinguish between "strong" and "weak" types of speech act depending on whether we have in view the performative (strong) act as Austin discusses it, or the descriptive (weak) act. There are conventions involved in both types, but in the latter case—of description—these conventions are mainly linguistic ones, concerning the conventional nature of meaning or language use in a given context. In the former case, all kinds of non-linguistic criteria are relevant. The Queen is to name the ship the "Titanic," but I steal in the night before and, smashing the champagne bottle on the hull, name it the "Wall Street." Alas, I am not so authorized, and the ship remains the "Titanic." That is a fact: the kind of fact we

5. Prominent figures on this path include Fish, *Text*; and Derrida, *Limited Inc.*

6. I have traced who developed what and how in Briggs, *Words in Action*, 31–143.

might call a "social fact," in other words a fact created by the agreement of certain relevant parties. A marriage contract, for example, as one of the most well-known of all examples of speech acts, creates the "social" fact of a marriage by the uttering of the words "I do" in the appropriate context(s). As a matter of brute fact, the ship, unlike Wall Street, goes down anyway. Speech acts can create social facts, but not brute ones, a distinction postmodern approaches in turn ignore to their (ocean-going) peril.[7]

In short, all speech acts are performative, but some are more performative than others. Philosophers who wish to sound a little more like Austin than Orwell render this claim as some are more *interesting* than others. Either way, this again clarifies the point that appealing to speech act theory does not involve a new grand-unified hermeneutical theory of everything, but is rather a way to highlight certain "performative uses" of language.

SPEECH ACT THEORY AS A MODEL FOR BIBLICAL INTERPRETATION

Acts performed by written texts are subject to at least the same array of interpretive possibilities as spoken ones. The above claims carry over to the written case: all texts may be speech acts in written form, but speech act theory will be an interesting hermeneutical option in those cases where "strong" speech acts occur, and where the facts in view are correspondingly "social."

One further possibility is perhaps introduced by the written form of speech acts: the notion that in construing a text we are basically being called upon to make some kind of interpretive judgment concerning the nature of the speech act. "I am with you always," says Jesus at the end of Matthew's Gospel. Do we read this (or construe it) as a statement or a promise? The two look the same of course, and in this case it hardly seems controversial, in context, to see the words as a promise. On reflection, many disputes of biblical interpretation turn on precisely this issue of construal: the text may be agreed but its performative force, or the kind of speech act it is, remains disputed. "It is well for a man not to touch a woman," says Paul in 1 Corinthians 7:1, using a euphemism for "have sex with." But is it Paul who advocates this? Is it irony? Is it a quotation of the Corinthians that he is about to reject? The words of the

---

7. The clearest discussion of this whole topic is Searle, *Construction of Social Reality*.

text may be clear, but which speech act is Paul performing?[8] In general, cases where the text itself invites or requires some kind of interpretive decision of this nature we may describe as cases of "strong construal," to distinguish again from the more general point that all words on a page require construal of some kind before they can be read or heard.

We are now in a position to make a proposal concerning a speech act hermeneutic. Texts that are strong speech acts need to be interpreted with reference to the various conventions they require, and these conventions will typically relate to non-linguistic states of affairs, in other words "the way things are in the world." In terms of biblical interpretation, biblical texts that operate as promises, blessings, praises, and so forth, invite a speech act approach, which will involve us having to "construe" the text in a certain way to see what it is *doing*, rather than just saying. In particular they require the reader to be invested or involved in the states of affairs that make the speech act work. It is not that this is an option for those who would like to feel particularly influenced by such texts. Rather, it is in the nature of the speech act concerned that it simply fails to function if the conventions are not satisfied.

For example, the confession that "Jesus is Lord,"[9] while it may perhaps function as a description of something (Jesus being Lord), is fundamentally doing much more than that. It is reflecting the conviction of the speaker—that the speaker takes a public stand on the issue of who Jesus is. As a confession, it is a performative speech act that creates (or recreates, or sustains, or modifies) the world in which the speaker stands under the lordship of Christ. Creeds perform the same function in churches today. Creeds do not (at least primarily) recite facts. They provide public testimony that the one reciting the creed adopts a stance in the public sphere of commitment to the consequences of confessing this faith. That this is true for creedal and confessional language, which remains a standard case of performative language, has often been recognized in what was generally the one theological area to be explored with reference to speech act theory, the area of liturgy and liturgical language.[10]

8. For the record, with most commentators, I suspect that Paul is quoting the Corinthians, who think they are quoting him in the first place, and he is about to suggest that they have not got this quite right.

9. See Romans 10:9; Philippians 2:11.

10. See for example Wainwright, "Language of Worship."

The use of scripture in liturgy, and indeed the reading of scripture as a liturgical act in the setting of a worship service, suggests that we are approaching here the area in which our interpreting of the Bible will overlap with such concerns. In fact, the wider concerns of the general theory of speech acts invite us to see liturgy as sitting at the "strong" end of the performative spectrum, and thus as one special case of what can be called a "hermeneutic of self-involvement." Markus Bockmuehl pinpoints the hermeneutical issue exactly when he says, "Without facing the inalienably transformative and self-involving demands that these ecclesial writings place on a serious reader, it is impossible to make significant sense of them."[11] How then should we best articulate the hermeneutic to which all this is pointing?

A HERMENEUTIC OF SELF-INVOLVEMENT

When someone says something like "God is my creator," this is not just a statement about God, but is a self-involving statement by the one who says it. A lot of biblical texts, or sayings, work like this. Significant speech about or in relation to God involves the speaker in a set of commitments in relationship to God and the rest of the created world. These commitments include matters of behavior and attitude as well as belief and action. If we take some such view of strong and weak speech acts and construal as we have sketched above, then such "self-involving speech acts" bind the speaker hermeneutically to the text and the rest of the world. Such a link is not always there. In the case of weak speech acts, for instance, it is not going to be particularly illuminating, if it is present at all. It is rather a function of particular types of speech act that involve conventions that, as it were, draw the speaker into the three-dimensional world of the text. In a hermeneutic of self-involvement, we invest ourselves in the text, and in the process we are changed—acted upon by its speech acts. When the speech acts are strong, and when the conventions are in place, the reader who wishes to understand the text has no option but to get involved.[12]

As an example of how a hermeneutic of self-involvement might operate, let us consider the speech act of forgiveness. We may tell ourselves,

11. Bockmuehl, *Seeing the Word*, 46.

12. For a full discussion of a "hermeneutic of self-involvement" see Briggs, *Words in Action*, 147–82.

"sticks and stones may break our bones, but words can never hurt me," but we clearly do so precisely because words possess just such a power.[13] However we are hurt, words similarly possess the potential for healing. But what act is performed when we say, "I forgive you," and what conventions are to be in place for such a (speech) act to be successful?

We will all be familiar with the difficulties of saying, "I forgive you." Typically we psychologize the issue and suggest that if we *feel* angry or bitter then we need to forgive, but who in such a situation has not experienced the frustration of working themselves up to utter the words "I forgive so-and-so," only to find that the feelings of anger and bitterness are unchanged the next day. Even to say, "I forgive you" face to face does not guarantee resolution. The key difference between a performative act such as saying, "I forgive you" and an utterance such as, "Today I will go for a walk" is that the first needs a strong degree of self-involvement in order to be successful. Even more so, anyone who successfully forgives must in fact be changed in who they are, or rather in their interpersonal relationships in the world, and this can only be effected through the performance of the speech act—by being "self-involved" in the performance. As I consider how I am to forgive, I realize that I must allow myself to be changed in the act of forgiving, otherwise I remain holding on to who I currently am, anger and all.

Thus the struggle and the reluctance to say, "I forgive you." It is an act that can only be performed by renegotiating one's social world and readmitting to it the one who has offended. Arguably this is a price too high to pay in some cases, but it is nevertheless what is at issue in many of the biblical discussions of forgiveness. Here the discussion is couched in terms of (re)admitting the sinner into "membership" of one's community, whether this be an official community such as a church or an informal one such as "the group of people with whom I am on speaking terms." In the case of the speech act of binding and loosing in Matthew 16:17–19, for example, Peter is given the "keys" which are, perhaps, to regulate precisely this aspect of forgiveness. But prior to the issue of membership is that of the stance of the one who is to forgive. A successful speech act of forgiveness requires the forgiver to reconstrue the world and in particular the relationship with the one to be forgiven. Various

---

13. The example comes from McClendon and Smith, *Convictions*, 19. Their discussion of speech act theory and religious language demonstrates another area again where there are benefits for theological concerns.

speech act discussions of forgiveness have concluded that fundamental to the act is the overcoming of resentment on the part of the forgiver. When Matthew 6:14–15 offers us the words of Jesus, "If you forgive others their trespasses, your heavenly Father will also forgive you; but if you do not forgive others, neither will your Father forgive your trespasses," what is at stake in the text is the willingness to waive one's right to be "repaid." To forgive I must reconstrue the world and my relationship with the offender. By learning this ability, I am moved from a world ruled by repayment and invested instead, through this self-involving speech act of forgiveness, in a different world, where my heavenly Father will construe my own deeds with the same reconfiguration of debt and pardon. It is not that God's forgiveness is offered after human forgiveness has taken place. Rather, I am myself remade in my involvement in the act of forgiveness, remade to be the kind of person who is forgiven by God.[14]

The hermeneutical bridge holds in this case, if hold it does, because forgiveness is a "strong" speech act. If I am not willing to invest in this text, then it will not change me, and I am back on the other side of the hermeneutical question, wondering how to "apply" these words of Jesus. When the words themselves are performative acts, then speech act theory articulates for us a better way, through a "hermeneutic of self-involvement."

THE SIGNIFICANCE OF SPEECH ACTS IN THE BIBLICAL NARRATIVE

Forgiving is just one speech act among many in the biblical narrative, but on reflection it is startling just how many highly significant speech acts there are, and in fact how much of the biblical story turns on "things done with words." The Eden story already involves acts of naming, commanding, interpreting, blaming and cursing, all of them acts performed with words. Before the book of Genesis is over, language has played a central role in the Babel story, in the negotiation of blessing between Isaac, Jacob and Esau, and in the form of covenantal promise to Abraham, with blessing and promising being almost the archetypal speech acts. Indeed, Anthony Thiselton has suggested that it is the notion of the biblical text as divine promise which best highlights the role that speech act theory can play as central to the nature of biblical hermeneutics.[15]

14. This example is considered in more detail in Briggs, *Words in Action*, 238–55.

15. Thiselton, "Communicative Action," 223–39.

Beyond Genesis, words and their power continue to predominate. The Ten Commandments are literally the "ten words"; the Psalms are acts of praise or lament, blessing or invocation; the words of the prophets announce judgment or vindication; the parables of Jesus spin their perplexing web around those with or without ears to hear; and early Christian preaching places speech once again central to the nature of Christian discourse. In all these contexts words occur in action, and not idling, left inactive in propositional statements. For too long biblical interpretation has been dominated by a model which has seen the biblical text as sentences carrying (static) meaning, meaning which then needs to be explained and applied in order to be understood. If our argument about self-involvement is correct, then we need to learn to see all these actions achieved by words as dynamic performances that require the reader of the Bible to be involved in what is going on.

Such involvement puts me in mind of the so-called "magic eye" pictures that were so popular a few years ago. These were typically brilliantly colored sheets of swirling and apparently inconsequential patterns, but once the viewer had learned to focus on the picture in a certain way it would become apparent that there was a three-dimensional object "hidden" within the pattern. The free-form shapes and swirls would give way to reveal a dolphin, or an oasis, or an airplane. But to a viewer who had not learned how to see the object, it remained an incomprehensible mystery. The ability to "see" the dolphin was at least in part a characteristic of the viewer, and required a kind of self-involvement with the picture. Crucially, to wring one more point out of this image, the "a-ha!" moment of "getting" the picture—the moment at which the construal of the object falls into place—is itself the moment of understanding, and no further translation of this understanding is necessary in order to apply it to the viewer.

To get involved with the speech acts of the biblical text is therefore a matter of learning how to be a reader or hearer who can construe these texts as performative actions. The potential payoff of such an approach correlates directly to the predominance of speech acts in the biblical narrative, and is therefore considerable. The risen Jesus in Acts 1:8, for example, promises—speech act—"you will be my witnesses in Jerusalem, in all Judea and Samaria, and to the ends of the earth." This is not basically evidence that Jesus had predictive power, and nor is it the obvious point that Luke wrote later on to reflect what ended up happening. Rather it relies on the idea that to witness is to perform a speech act of testifying to (in this case) Jesus: both reporting on what has been seen, heard, and experienced as well as taking a public stand on it, vouching for its reliability, relevance, and so forth. Who will do this? It is the kind of people who have understood who Jesus is, an understanding that will fall fully into place only "when the Holy Spirit has come upon you." At that point, Acts 1:8 suggests, Jesus' listeners will have "construed" Jesus according to the way he wished to be understood. In articulating this new understanding they will be testifying to its truth. Jesus' speech act is thus a promise to all those (self-)involved in paying attention to who he is, whereas to all those standing back and watching the propositions process by, it appears to be some form of statement with a future reference. Preached in such a flat way today as a biblical text it threatens to reduce to the kind of sermon which turns the gospel word of life into simply a commandment to "go out and evangelize," a work the weight of which hangs heavy on most of its hearers as anything but the word of life. And there is an abundance of such examples where a speech act analysis draws out the inner "logic" (or as philosophers often say, the "grammar") of what is going on.

THE WORD IN ACTION: GOD'S INVOLVEMENT WITH CREATION

Finally it is worth noting that all that has been said so far really pertains to the speech acts performed in and by the biblical text in terms of human authors and characters in the narrative. In addition to all the various possibilities opened up by speech act theory in such cases, there is also the wider issue of the performative nature of the Word of God itself, and the extent to which speech act considerations can help us to reflect on the nature and doctrine of scripture too.[16]

These two broad kinds of issue meet in the area of specific divine speech acts in scripture. Francis Watson has even drawn attention to creation as a speech act: what he calls "the speech act model of divine creativity." At least on days one and three (verses 3, 9, and 11) of the Genesis 1 account, there appears to be no intermediate act between God commanding, "Let there be . . ." and its being so.[17] Such a divine

16. As we saw in chapter 8 above. I have reviewed this set of issues in Briggs, "Speech-Act Theory" (2005).

17. Watson, *Text, Church and World*, 140–51, especially 140–42 where he compares this model with "fabrication" and "mediation" models.

speech act suggests God's own self-involvement with the resultant creation, and as the Christian doctrine of creation has always maintained, it is on our own parts a self-involving act to construe the world in which we live as creation.

To see biblical texts as performative actions, and to see the biblical text as the Word of God in action: two different reasons for getting involved with speech act theory in the many and various hermeneutical tasks of biblical interpretation.

11

Transformation

How Scripture Forms the Reader

IN THIS CHAPTER WE consider some further angles on the question of how scripture forms and/or transforms the reader. We have seen throughout our discussion that biblical studies will have spiritual and theological dimensions alongside many other aspects. In the context of Christian ministry, biblical studies also finds itself pressed into service to have something to say on all manner of practical and pastoral issues, and in one sense, rightly so. However the differing agendas of biblical studies as a discipline, as compared to the demands of church ministry, sometimes result in the scriptural voice seeming somewhat distant from our immediate concerns. I shall suggest that this conundrum is not easily resolved in terms of simply making biblical studies "more practical." I shall then look at how concentrating on interpreting the Bible on its own terms, in so far as that is possible, is the surest way ahead for letting it do its formational and transformational work. This will involve brief reflection on the purpose of having "scripture" at all, and then an attempt to explore one or two examples. Sadly, this chapter will not entirely practice what it preaches, and therefore I cannot claim that anyone who follows the argument will be either formed or transformed, but hopefully it will be at least a step in the right direction.

A TALE OF TWO AGENDAS

In 1970, James Smart wrote a wonderful little book entitled *The Strange Silence of the Bible in the Church*. He noted the discomforting fact that increased attention to hermeneutics—the book was subtitled "A Study in Hermeneutics"—had actually gone hand in hand with a general decline in the church's attention to scripture itself. In a closing "practical post-script" he memorably described the transition undertaken by a student stepping out into the wide world of Christian ministry:

> He goes from a situation in which he has the support and en-
> couragement of professors and fellow students, and, not least, of
> a well-stocked library, to a situation where, once his fellow minis-
> ters have installed him, he finds himself very much alone. When
> he attends the district governing body to which he belongs, its
> sessions are likely to be wholly occupied with church business
> and to have no time for discussion of such matters as Biblical
> interpretation or theological issues. . . . It is not surprising that for
> many pastors the theological interest fails to survive, with serious
> consequences for the character of their ministry.[1]

Approaches to biblical interpretation have changed in many ways in the intervening years, but has this scenario changed much with regard to the transition from study into ministry? If we might no longer speak of "the strange silence of the Bible in the church," it is perhaps troubling that Stephen Pattison's widely cited *A Critique of Pastoral Care* offers simply a more focused updating of the same problem:

> The Bible is appealed to and consulted in all matters of Christian
> life. It is regarded as authoritative and indispensable. No one,
> then, could say that it is not important; but if they were relying
> on the contemporary literature of pastoral care, they might well
> draw the opposite conclusion. . . . There is an almost absolute
> and embarrassing silence about the Bible in pastoral care theory.[2]

As it happens, Pattison's own text is one of the primary triggers of doing something about this state of affairs, although the fact that this quote is taken from the third edition of his book, as recently as 2000, suggests that progress has been slow. And even where there has been progress,

---

1. Smart, *Strange Silence*, 168.
2. Pattison, *Critique*, 106.

the framework presupposed by the discussion is that there are two agendas at work: that of the Bible, and that of the pastoral minister.

Although there has been increasing attention to this matter from the "pastoral" side, the main contribution from the biblical studies side is a book now almost forty years old, Walter Wink's explosive little 1973 tract, *The Bible in Human Transformation*. This, as any who read it will doubtless not forget in a hurry, opened up with the claim that historical criticism was bankrupt, not in the sense that it should now be proclaimed dead and buried, but in the sense that it had become "incapable of achieving what most of its practitioners considered its purpose to be: so to interpret the Scriptures that the past becomes alive and illumines our present with new possibilities for personal and social transformation."[3] Among the various ways forward Wink explores, most prominent is a psychoanalytic model for an approach of questioning the text to lay bare "the truth of our own personal and social being," leading to a renewed emphasis on communion.[4] Wink followed this with a practically orientated book, *Transforming Bible Study*, which sought to draw out psychological insights for exegesis. There he states, "Our goal then is so to move among these mighty texts that we are transformed."[5] It is not that nobody has pursued this line of thought in the years since Wink wrote. Indeed I suspect that there is much good will on both sides of the pastoral/biblical divide to see transformation rooted in scripture and effective in the reader's life, but people often seem to be stuck when it comes to working out what it will mean in practice.

We will use a few examples to tease out the issues. I recall once attending a seminar at a Christian leadership conference on the topic of delegation. The speaker wanted to begin with a biblical example, which he felt would be a matter of letting the Bible set some kind of agenda for the seminar. As it happened, he picked a fairly poor example: Jesus sending out the seventy in Luke 10, where verse 1 turned out to represent the principle that you should not delegate anything you would be unwilling to do yourself. Arguably he could have picked Jethro counseling Moses

3. Wink, *Human Transformation*, 2.

4. Ibid., 64.

5. Wink, *Transforming*, 42. There is a problem with Wink's specific argument that I shall indirectly address later, but in essence it is this: he sees transformation as attainable by switching from historical-critical categories to psychologically orientated ones, and this, in my judgment, does not get to the heart of the matter, for reasons to be explored.

that he would wear himself out if he did not teach other people how to judge disputes (Exodus 19:18), and perhaps that would have been a better example. But with either passage, what real role could the biblical passage possibly have played in this seminar, since the subject matter of the seminar was set from elsewhere? It involved principles of delegation well attested in all manner of leadership and management literature, Christian and non-Christian.

For a second example we return to the topic of forgiveness that we explored in the previous chapter. It is surely a supremely pressing pastoral issue as to how we should think about and practice forgiveness. The biblical scholar will be well placed to offer, say, an analysis of forgiveness in Matthew's Gospel as a key to Matthew's idea of how Christian communities should understand membership in the community. Meanwhile the pastor is trying to address a wide range of instances in which forgiveness is at issue. The prescriptions of Matthew 18 concerning how to try to win back a brother who sins against you, and how many times to forgive him, will address some of these situations, but by no means all. We are perhaps all familiar with the glum conclusion of the imagined discussion here: the Bible does not really address the issue about which the minister is asking. But in this case we see that there is *some* overlap of the concerns of biblical studies and pastoral practice, and the task might be described as the need to discern how and when that overlap occurs.

For a third example, consider a passage such as Romans 12 (though this is not as random a choice as it may appear, for reasons that will become clearer later). We might perhaps look at verses 9–21 with their discussion of genuine love, mutual affection, blessing those who persecute you, living peaceably with all, and overcoming evil with good. None of this appears to be conceptually difficult, and it is easy to imagine lifting it straight off the page and presenting it as practical wisdom for the Christian life to any member of one's congregation, if not to any person at all. Now if we are to imagine pastoral practice putting its agenda to the biblical scholar—"How should I treat those who persecute me?"—then surely here is an example where the agendas overlap, and a meaningful response might be made from one discipline to another.

Perhaps you can tell from the way that I have set up this example that I do not think this is right. Why not? The problem lies with the habit, deeply ingrained across the theological spectrum, of reading off an agenda from the surface of the text that happens to fit very neatly into a system of values already believed. In this case, Romans 12 offers a powerful exhortation to love, and ties in with a view one comes across very often in churches of all types: that being a Christian is all about being loved by God, and learning to love God and neighbor in return. Love, in the terms of our own discussion, becomes the fundamental hermeneutical category within which the text is understood, assessed, and then, to a greater or lesser extent, implemented.

We may do well to call to mind at this point the delightful warning offered by Samuel Taylor Coleridge: "The main hindrance to the use of the scriptures . . . lies in the notion that you are already acquainted with its contents."[6] Admittedly, these days, I would rather say that this is one main hindrance, since there is another obvious hindrance to the use of the scriptures today, which is the staggering *lack* of acquaintance with its contents exhibited in so much Christian thinking. But be that as it may, Coleridge's point has never been clearer with respect to hermeneutical frameworks. If we rush to assume that we already know which categories are the right ones to bring to the biblical text in order to pursue the questions we already have, then we shall assuredly miss the ways in which the biblical witness to the God of Abraham, Isaac, and Jacob, and the God of our Lord Jesus Christ, seeks to reshape our concerns around an agenda which we do not naturally possess (and are unlikely to learn from the culture in which we live).

In this particular case, love as basic hermeneutical category starts to look quite interesting around Romans 12:20. Verse 19 quotes Deuteronomy 32:35 to remind us that "Vengeance is mine, I will repay, says the Lord." Verse 20 then takes up the point of this citation by quoting Proverbs 25:21–22: "If your enemies are hungry, feed them; if they are thirsty, give them something to drink; for by doing this you will heap burning coals on their heads."[7] What do commentators make of this? Some argue that what Paul has in mind here is the inflicting of "such an inward sense of shame as will either lead him [the enemy] to real contrition and to being no more an enemy but a friend, or else, if he refuses to be reconciled, will remain with him as the pain of a bad conscience."[8]

6. From Coleridge's *The Statesman's Manual*, 1816; cited by Watson, "Coleridge," 125.

7. In fact the precise quotation is from the Septuagint (LXX) of Proverbs, though it makes relatively little difference.

8. Cranfield, *Romans*, 649.

Others suggest that "heaping coals of fire" on someone's head must have had some kind of positive sense,[9] perhaps from an Egyptian repentance ritual—where carrying coals of fire (in a dish) on one's head symbolized repentance.[10] Often the two explanations are merged,[11] perhaps in the hope that at least one of them will turn out to work.

What has happened here is that a hermeneutical impulse to pursue some less intuitive level of understanding has kicked in because on the surface these two verses seem to jar with a framework hitherto easily understood. But this is to fall foul of the ever-present protest regarding the role of hermeneutics in biblical interpretation, which is that it is in the end nothing more than a sophisticated form of self-legitimation for getting round the bits of scripture that we do not like. But as we have seen throughout, hermeneutics is a general phenomenon relevant to the handling of all texts, and is not a form of interpretive cavalry riding to the rescue only when there is a problem.

The heart of the hermeneutical issue is that if we bring to the text our own understanding of the category of "love," and use it as the basis for adopting this text for moral exhortation and encouragement, then we shall inevitably twist the passage to serve an agenda driven by our own understanding of love. What one needs to do is to learn what the category of "love" is from the biblical witness if one wants to let this text operate with its own agenda. It is on the level of hermeneutical categories that the problem of clashing agendas plays out.

Now who would dispute the great value of cherishing the importance of love, and surely this is a quality to which a Christian above all should aspire without getting tangled up in worrying about defining it? If our argument so far is right, the answer to this last question, which is more usually posed rhetorically, is "almost, but not quite," for it makes a great deal of difference if we replace the biblical categories with similar looking ones that are at home in our own privatized and late-capitalist society. Ironically, what happens with a category like "love" is that it is held to be self-evident as to what it is, and this self-evident concept is then used as a standard against which to judge those parts of scripture felt not to measure up to it. Those who, in Coleridge's terms, "already know" that the Bible is all about love will duly find themselves creating a

---

9. Dunn, *Romans*, 750–51.

10. Cf. Klassen, "Coals of Fire."

11. Wright, "Romans," 714–15.

self-fulfilling canon within the canon, which does little more than reflect back out to the interpreter the very values he or she went in with. But now there is the added complication that all sorts of passages have to be reinterpreted or simply dropped because they do not measure up. One does not have to spend long on this path before beginning to wonder whether it would not be a whole lot easier to dispense with the troublesome work of interpreting scripture for moral formation and transformation, and simply jump straight to the categories offered by the many other resources to hand for this task. And this path is of course widely taken in practice, as witnessed in the considerable success, in Christian circles, of concepts such as "the purpose-driven life," or the considerable prevalence, in Christian sermons, of exhortations to do good and live a moral life.

In staying at the appealing end of the moral spectrum (by focusing on a category such as love, or peace and loving kindness, or indeed formation and transformation) I hope to help us realize that the hermeneutical question in interpreting the Bible is not how to negotiate between the inspiring and the problematic bits. Rather it is to force us to come up with a more profound reason for persevering with scripture than the simple fact that it does have plenty of inspiring bits. The inspiration which it affords, in other words, is a byproduct of scripture's own agenda, which lies elsewhere, and which sees scripture as something other than an end in itself. I am reminded of Gerhard von Rad's wonderful quote to a preaching class: "I give you about ten to twenty beginners' sermons, in which you will repeat what you have learned. Then you will have preached yourselves out. Then if you do not make the discovery that every text wants to speak for itself, you are lost."[12]

READING SCRIPTURE ON ITS OWN TERMS

In earlier chapters we have explored the notion that to read scripture on its own terms is to let God set a God-centered agenda for the best part of all our thinking, questioning, and acting. Consider the startling confession of Dietrich Bonhoeffer, made in the latter part of his life, after, significantly, he had had the experience of running the seminary at Finkenwalde for the Confessing Church, where matters of personal formation and transformation impressed themselves upon him with a

12. Von Rad, *Biblical Interpretation*, 18.

very great urgency. In a letter written in 1936, Bonhoeffer had this to say: "I want to confess quite simply that I believe the Bible alone is the answer to all our questions, and that we only need to ask persistently and with some humility in order to receive an answer from it."[13] Now perhaps this is written with a certain hyperbole, and some do suggest that Bonhoeffer is endlessly quotable because one can to an extent turn his words to support a rather wide range of theological positions. After all, surely not *all* our questions are answered by the Bible, not even all our serious questions, nor even all our theological questions. But in his emphasis on persistence and humility, Bonhoeffer perhaps suggests that in our own serious engagement with scripture, we shall come to ask better, more probing, and more profound questions, which, he goes on to say, will penetrate to the God who lies beneath the surface of the text.[14] It is these questions, he urges, that will indeed turn out to be answered by scripture. This is a claim, then, that we should be learning to ask the questions which are put to us by scripture, to read it, as literary critics like to say, "with the grain" rather than "against the grain," and that by so doing we shall find ourselves in a better, or wiser, or more spiritually and theologically enriching, place.

But what does this mean in practice? What does it mean for questions of formation and transformation? How does the Bible in practice play a role in forming its readers? Let us turn to some passages where scripture presents itself as formative or transformative. Perhaps our question then should be: is "formation" or "transformation" the hermeneutical category appropriate to reading scripture on its own terms?

There are many places in scripture where the agenda seems to be explicitly concerned with matters of transformation. Most obviously, Romans 12:2, "Do not be conformed to this world, but be transformed by the renewing of your minds, so that you may discern what is the will of God—what is good and acceptable and perfect."

This verse lay behind the earlier choice of Romans 12 as a potentially self-evident passage about love. The other line of argument one could have raised against that view was the unforgettable presence of a

13. Bonhoeffer, *Meditating*, 43, from a letter dated April 8, 1936. Also cited in Bonhoeffer, *Reflections*, 1, as "I believe that the Bible alone is the answer to all our questions and that to receive an answer from it, we only need to ask with persistence and a little courage."

14. Bonhoeffer, *Meditating*, 44.

"therefore" in verse 1. Presumably, in Paul's logic, all this talk of love is consequent to some preceding argument, which here in verse 2 appears to play the role of transforming us by the renewing of our minds. This is bad news for those who wish to cut straight to the practical payoff.

This verse also suggests that it would be a mistake to draw some kind of distinction between "formation" and "transformation" in terms of spiritual growth developed inwardly, as it were, and growth brought about from "outside." What does the "trans-" in transformation signify here, in the same Greek word from which we get "metamorphosis"? It is reshaping[15] driven by the renewal of the mind, which presumably is achieved by way of engaging with what has been argued in chapters 1–11 leading up to the "therefore." This mystery of the revelation of God (Romans 16:25–26), this disclosure of a righteousness of/from God "apart from law" (3:21), revealed "from faith to faith" (1:17), and declared with power in the resurrection (1:4)—it is wrestling with this revelation which will renew the mind and bring about transformation. The crowd of witnesses who have done this (with Romans) is an impressive list indeed, and on a much smaller, more personal note, it is probably struggling with Romans that has brought about my own most profound transformation in terms of engaging with who God is. Now of course there is the hermeneutical question—the move to suspicion— the dispassionate willingness to follow Paul for eleven (or even sixteen) chapters and then step back and say "Well, is this argument (of Paul's) any good?" But "good" according to which criteria, or whose tradition? Whose concept of love, or liberation, or justice, will trump Paul's, as he wends his way from the gospel promised beforehand in the Holy Scriptures (1:2) to the first female apostle (16:7)? There are of course candidates, but are they transformative ones?

This same concept of transformation turns up in 2 Corinthians 3:18. It is a self-involving concept of experiencing the glory of God, rather like Moses experienced, such that "one cannot see such glory and come away unchanged: to experience God's glory in Jesus Christ is to undergo a transformation 'into the same image.'"[16] And although the word is different,[17] the idea recurs in Philippians 3:10, where Paul talks

15. Or "re-schematizing," as the parallel word *suschēmatizesthe*—"conformed"— might have it.

16. Barclay, "2 Corinthians," 1360.

17. It is in fact *symmorphizō*, a word which combines the prefixes and roots of the

of "becoming like" Christ (NRSV)—or being "conformed" to Christ—by way of "knowing Christ and the power of his resurrection and the fellowship of his sufferings."

If this is true, then transformation, in New Testament terms, is what happens when we know God, in Christ. The experience of the revelation of God is transformative, in that it is a self-involving concept which reconstitutes the recipient. This notion of transformation is specifically focused on a person's removal from one sphere of influence—variously described, but basically the power of sin—and relocation into another sphere of influence—the power of Christ and his resurrection. The goal is growth toward a goal: conformity (that word again, *symmorphous*) to the image of God's Son (Romans 8:29).

The categories of formation and transformation as they are presented to us in scripture are to be understood in terms of a concept equally controlled in the New Testament by the idea of "conformation"—into the image of Christ. This conformation is achieved through the experience of the revelation of God. As we read scripture, therefore, our goal must be to try to read it in accord with its own agenda, as God's self-revelation. In this way, it will in fact do its practical, pastoral, and deeply personal transforming work.

Given the measure of continuity between how God has spoken "in these last days" and how he spoke "long ago . . . to our ancestors, in many and various ways by the prophets" (Hebrews 1:1), we might expect to find that incidents of reading scripture that are recorded in scripture itself offer hints that the reading of scripture effects transformation. I think this is so, though this is not the place to go through a long list of examples. Obvious cases for consideration include the impact of the reading of the book of the law in the time of Josiah, or its reading in the time of Ezra and Nehemiah upon the return to Jerusalem, or Daniel's study of the book of Jeremiah.

We may for now note the simple confidence of Psalm 1: meditation upon the Torah day and night will, like the tree planted by streams of water, produce fruit in season. This is an image of transformation that envisages the interpreter being changed by persistent encounter with God's self-revelation in the Torah.

---

two terms used in Romans 12:2. I owe this observation to Wright, "Romans," 705 n. 489.

Our job is not to create, out of the biblical materials, a God we find acceptable, by fitting God into the categories we hold to be self-evidently appropriate for a deity. It is not God who is to be transformed by our hermeneutical endeavor. Rather *we* are to be transformed, in fact conformed, into the image of the Son of God, the God who is revealed in the whole canon, and not just in those sections that inspire us (nor even, for that matter, just those sections that trouble us). As with so many virtues in life, such as happiness, joy, and peace, we do not arrive at transformation by aiming for it. In our biblical study, as Christian readers, we seek the God of Abraham, Isaac, and Jacob, the God revealed in these last days in Jesus Christ. In thus pursuing the biblical agenda, we too shall, though neither in a flash nor the twinkling of an eye, be changed.

12

The Word of Life and the Pursuit of Wisdom

This book has been based on the idea that our goal in reading the Bible is to read it wisely: to have eyes to see. Like Eliot's wise men, that can be a disconcerting experience, but it is one that allows scripture to come alive for us and capture something of the creative energy of the Word of God lurking within it. That the Bible remains to so many a dull and boring book is one of the greatest sadnesses of the modern church, where making sure that we think the right thing has sometimes been more important than opening our eyes to see just what is going on in scripture.

It seems only fair to offer a short "concluding hermeneutical postscript" by way of a brief attempt to say what wisdom is, and to look at one place where scripture encourages us to pursue it. I would like to suggest that one key element of wisdom, in biblical perspective, is the ability to see the world as God would have us see it. It involves revelation, and it involves being given eyes to see. To my mind, one of the most significant verses of Proverbs is 20:12, "The hearing ear and the seeing eye—the Lord has made them both." This suggests that true sight, indeed "insight," comes from God. The wise reader will therefore seek, in their reading, to have their eyes opened—a passive construction taken up, famously, in Luke 24:31 on the road to Emmaus ("their eyes were opened"), as we saw at the beginning of this book. If wisdom is, at least in part, the ability to see rightly, then Proverbs 20:12 suggests the very ability to see anything at all, in the morally significant sense of discernment, is a gift of the Lord.

The wise readers, then, are to develop wise habits of reading scripture that will allow them to discern "God's breath" in it, and see the appropriate ways in which it speaks to them today. All of this practical wisdom involves investing in the technical abilities to read the biblical text in historical and literary context, with all the challenges and rewards that this revealed in our earlier chapters. Above all, for the Christian reader, it is to read the Bible always on the road to Emmaus, always in a hermeneutical circle (or spiral) of interaction between Christ and the scriptures. By way of a conclusion that holds all these ideas together under the heading of "Reading the Bible Wisely," let us turn briefly to the letter of James.

James sometimes gets a bad press among theologians. It is known for being the book that says, "faith without works is dead'" (James 2:17), although that is by no means entirely representative of its teaching. In many ways it is the book in the New Testament most concerned with wisdom.

Near the beginning, James offers the following advice: "If any of you is lacking in wisdom, ask God, who gives to all generously and ungrudgingly, and it will be given you" (1:5). This seems simple enough, and who would not then ask for it and . . . become wise? There must be a catch. In fact the catch is stated immediately, so it hardly counts as small print. Here it is: "But ask in faith, never doubting" (1:6), since the one who doubts is nothing less than "double-minded" and "unstable in every way." At first sight that does seem harsh. It can also in practice lead to the awful experience of trying ever harder to pray for something by mustering up enough faith to *really* believe that it will happen—a defeating and downward-spiraling experience if ever there was one. Surely there must be some other way to understand this passage?

Perhaps the answer lies in reflecting on the nature of wisdom here. What happens if we pursue the idea that wisdom is seeing things how God wants us to see them? I think we can discern that there is a reason why we must believe that God can answer our prayer when we pray for wisdom. The reason is that a God who can make us wise is one aspect of the world we must see in order to be wise. If we doubt that God can do it, then we are imagining a world that is not the world God wants us to see. Thus, in a sense, this particular self-involving prayer request is a self-fulfilling one. If we can be the sort of person who can pray it, then it is already answered for us—or, in James' words, God will give generously to all who ask it. If we pray it the wrong way, it cannot possibly work. This does not resolve all the interpretive questions about those prayers in the New Testament where sufficient faith is the requirement, and it does not mean that doubt does not have a proper place in certain situations, but for this particular prayer, for wisdom from God, it explains the qualifications that James puts on it.[1]

This very ability to see the world this way is actually there right at the start of James, in the startling verse that exhorts us, "Whenever you face trials of any kind consider it nothing but joy" (1:2). The ability to see a trial as a joy is not a characteristic of the trial we are going through, but of ourselves and whether or not we have eyes to see.

James is rightly known as a practical letter. It appeals to many readers for that reason. In 1:21 we read, "Rid yourselves of all sordidness and rank growth of wickedness, and welcome with meekness the implanted word that has the power to save your souls." There can be few readers who would not wish to do precisely what this verse says. But how? How can one rid oneself of all that is wicked within? Is this our own work? Again, the answer is "yes and no." We are to receive, says James, the implanted word within us. What word is that? As we look back over the preceding passage, we come across a pair of verses that go right to the heart of our whole topic of reading the Bible wisely. Wisdom, life, and release from sin: these are all gifts of the God who is the giver of every good and perfect gift (1:17). This is the God who gave us birth by the "word of truth" (1:18). To receive salvation, or life, or to rid ourselves of what is rotten within us, is to hold on to the word of truth.

This word of truth may be understood as the same word which is elsewhere called the "word of life," or which is characterized as the "Word of God" in various places in scripture. To be wise, then, is to know that any insight we have is from God, and that any time we see with wise eyes, these eyes are the gift of God. It is the reminder that by ourselves we are unable to attain wisdom, but that if we cease trying to persuade God that we deserve the gift, then he will be pleased to remind us that it is ours anyway. In James' language: if we confess our "sordidness and wickedness," then he reminds us that he has given us birth by his word of truth.

---

1. A form of this argument goes back to Kierkegaard. I learned it from Polk, *Biblical Kierkegaard*, 121–25.

Wisdom is not a cheap option. According to Proverbs 4:7 it will cost all we have. "Whatever else you get, get insight," says that particular proverb. That insight is the wisdom to see the world as God wants us to see it. In hermeneutical terms: the wisdom to read the Bible as God would have us read it, with open eyes. Or more precisely: with eyes opened, just like the disciples on the road to Emmaus.

Bibliography

Alter, Robert, and Frank Kermode, eds. *The Literary Guide to the Bible*. London: Collins, 1987.

Athas, George. *The Tel Dan Inscription: A Reappraisal and a New Interpretation*. Journal for the Study of the Old Testament Supplement Series 360. Sheffield: Sheffield Academic, 2003.

———. "Setting the Record Straight: What Are We Saying about the Tel Dan Inscription?" *Journal of Semitic Studies* 51 (2006) 241–55.

Austin, J. L. *How to Do Things with Words*. Edited by J. O. Urmson and Marina Sbisa. 1962. 2nd ed. Oxford: Oxford University Press, 1975.

Barclay, John. "2 Corinthians." In *Eerdmans Commentary on the Bible*, edited by J. D. G. Dunn and J. W. Rogerson, 1353–73. Grand Rapids: Eerdmans, 2003.

Barth, Karl. "The Strange New World within the Bible." In *The Word of God and the Word of Man*, 28–50. London: Hodder & Stoughton, 1928.

Barton, John. *Making the Christian Bible*. London: Dartman, Longman & Todd, 1997.

Bauckham, Richard. *The Climax of Prophecy: Studies on the Book of Revelation*. Edinburgh: T. & T. Clark, 1993.

———. *The Theology of the Book of Revelation*. New Testament Theology. Cambridge: Cambridge University Press, 1993.

Beckwith, Roger T. "Toward a Theology of the Biblical Text." In *Doing Theology for the People of God: Studies in Honour of J. I. Packer*, edited by Donald Lewis and Alister McGrath, 43–50. Leicester: Apollos, 1996.

Bloesch, Donald G. *Holy Scripture: Revelation, Inspiration & Interpretation*. Christian Foundations 2. Downers Grove, IL: InterVarsity, 1994.

Bockmuehl, Markus. *Seeing the Word: Refocusing New Testament Study*. Studies in Theological Interpretation. Grand Rapids: Baker Academic, 2006.

Bonhoeffer, Dietrich. *Meditating on The Word*. Cambridge, MA: Cowley, 1986.

———. *Reflections on the Bible*. Peabody, MA: Hendrickson, 2004.

Briggs, Richard S. "Getting Involved: Speech Acts and Biblical Interpretation." *Anvil* 20 (2003) 25–34.

———. *Reading Isaiah: A Beginner's Guide*. Grove Biblical Series B55. Cambridge: Grove, 2010.

———. "The Role of the Bible in Formation and Transformation: A Hermeneutical and Theological Analysis." *Anvil* 24 (2007) 167–82.

————. "Speech-Act Theory." In *Dictionary for Theological Interpretation of the Bible*, edited by Kevin J. Vanhoozer et al., 763–66. Grand Rapids: Baker Academic; and London: SPCK, 2005.

————. "Speech-Act Theory." In *Words and the Word: Explorations in Biblical Interpretation and Literary Theory*, edited by David G. Firth and Jamie A. Grant, 75–110. Nottingham: Apollos, 2008.

————. *Words in Action: Speech Act Theory and Biblical Interpretation*. Edinburgh: T. & T. Clark, 2001.

————. *Why Read the Old Testament?* Grove Biblical Series B60. Cambridge: Grove, 2011.

Brueggemann, Walter. *Isaiah 1–39*. Westminster Bible Companions. Louisville: Westminster John Knox, 1997.

————. *Old Testament Theology: An Introduction*. Library of Biblical Theology. Nashville: Abingdon, 2008.

————. *Texts Under Negotiation: The Bible and Postmodern Imagination*. Minneapolis: Fortress, 1993.

————. *Theology of the Old Testament. Testimony, Dispute, Advocacy*. Minneapolis: Fortress, 1997.

Campenhausen, Hans von. *The Formation of the Christian Bible*. Translated by J. A. Baker. Philadelphia: Fortress, 1972.

Carr, David M. "Reading Isaiah from Beginning (Isaiah 1) to End (Isaiah 65–66): Multiple Modern Possibilities." In *New Visions of Isaiah*, edited by Roy F. Melugin and Marvin A. Sweeney, 188–218. Journal for the Study of the Old Testament Supplement Series 214. Sheffield: Sheffield Academic, 1996.

Chapman, Stephen B. "Reclaiming Inspiration for the Bible." In *Canon and Biblical Interpretation*, edited by Craig Bartholomew et al., 167–206. Scripture and Hermeneutics Series 7. Grand Rapids: Zondervan and Carlisle: Paternoster, 2006.

Childs, Brevard S. *The Church's Guide for Reading Paul: The Canonical Shaping of the Pauline Corpus*. Grand Rapids: Eerdmans, 2008.

————. *Introduction to the Old Testament as Scripture*. Philadelphia: Fortress, 1979.

Clines, David J. A. *What Does Eve Do to Help? And Other Readerly Questions to the Old Testament*. Journal for the Study of the Old Testament Supplement Series 94. Sheffield: JSOT Press, 1990.

Cranfield, C.E.B. *The Epistle to the Romans: Vol 2*. International Critical Commentary. Edinburgh: T. & T. Clark, 1979.

Davis, Ellen F., and Richard B. Hays, eds. *The Art of Reading Scripture*. Grand Rapids: Eerdmans, 2003.

Derrida, Jacques. *Limited Inc*. Edited by Gerald Graff. Evanston, IL: Northwestern University Press, 1988.

Dunn, James D. G. *Romans 9–16*. Word Biblical Commentary 38B. Waco: Word, 1988.

Eliot, T. S. "Journey of the Magi." In *The Complete Poems and Plays*, 103–4. London: Faber and Faber, 1969.

Exum, J. Cheryl. *Tragedy and Biblical Narrative: Arrows of the Almighty*. Cambridge: Cambridge University Press, 1992.

Fish, Stanley. *Is There a Text in This Class? The Authority of Interpretive Communities*. Cambridge, MA: Harvard University Press, 1980.

Ford, David F. *Christian Wisdom. Desiring God and Learning in Love*. Cambridge Studies in Christian Doctrine 16. Cambridge: Cambridge University Press, 2007.

———. *A Long Rumour of Wisdom: Redescribing Theology*. Cambridge: Cambridge University Press, 1992.

Fowl, Stephen E. *Theological Interpretation of Scripture*. Cascade Companions. Eugene, OR: Cascade, 2009.

Funk, Robert W., and Roy W. Hoover, eds. *The Five Gospels: The Search for the Authentic Words of Jesus*. New York: Macmillan, 1993.

Gadamer, Hans-Georg. *Truth and Method*. 1975. 2nd ed. London: Sheed & Ward, 1989.

Gaventa, Beverly Roberts, and Richard B. Hays, eds. *Seeking the Identity of Jesus: A Pilgrimage*. Grand Rapids: Eerdmans, 2008.

Gooding, David. *According to Luke: A New Exposition of the Third Gospel*. Leicester: InterVarsity, 1987.

Green, Joel B. *1 Peter*. Two Horizons New Testament Commentary. Grand Rapids: Eerdmans, 2007.

———. *The Gospel of Luke*. New International Commentary on the New Testament. Grand Rapids: Eerdmans, 1997.

Hauerwas, Stanley. *Unleashing the Scripture: Freeing the Bible from Captivity to America*. Nashville: Abingdon, 1993.

Kähler, Martin. *The So-Called Historical Jesus and the Historic, Biblical Christ*. 1896. Reprint, Philadelphia: Fortress, 1964.

Kaiser, Otto. *The Old Testament Apocrypha: An Introduction*. Peabody, MA: Hendrickson, 2004.

Kelsey, David H. "The Bible and Christian Theology." *Journal of the American Academy of Religion* 48 (1980) 385–402.

———. *Proving Doctrine: The Uses of Scripture in Modern Theology*. Harrisburg, PA: Trinity, 1999. Reprint of *The Uses of Scripture in Recent Theology*. Philadelphia: Fortress, 1975.

Klassen, W. "Coals of Fire: Signs of Repentance or Revenge?" *New Testament Studies* 9 (1962–63) 337–50.

Lash, Nicholas. *Seeing in the Dark*. London: Dartman, Longman & Todd, 2005.

Lewis, C.S. *Reflections on the Psalms*. New York and London: Harcourt Brace Jovanovich, 1958.

MacIntyre, Alasdair. *Whose Justice? Which Rationality?* Notre Dame: University of Notre Dame Press, 1988.

McClendon Jr., James Wm., and James M. Smith. *Convictions: Defusing Religious Relativism*. Valley Forge, PA: Trinity, 1994.

McDonald, Lee Martin. *The Biblical Canon. Its Origin, Transmission, and Authority*. Peabody, MA: Hendrickson, 2007.

Miles, Jack. *God: A Biography*. New York: Vintage, 1996.

The Mishnah: A New Translation. Translated by Jacob Neusner. New Haven, and London: Yale University Press, 1988.

Moberly, R. W. L. *The Bible, Theology and Faith: A Study of Abraham and Jesus*. Cambridge Studies in Christian Doctrine 5. Cambridge: Cambridge University Press, 2000.

Motyer, Steve. *Antisemitism and the New Testament*. Grove Biblical Series B23. Cambridge: Grove, 2002.

Moule, C. F. D. *Forgiveness and Reconciliation*. London: SPCK, 1998.

Pattison, Stephen. *A Critique of Pastoral Care*. 1988. 3rd ed. London: SCM, 2000.

Polk, Timothy Houston. *The Biblical Kierkegaard: Reading by the Rule of Faith*. Macon, GA: Mercer University Press, 1997.

Rad, Gerhard von. *Biblical Interpretations in Preaching.* Translated by John E. Seely. Nashville: Abingdon, 1977.

————. *The Message of the Prophets.* London: SCM, 1968.

Rowland, Christopher. *Revelation.* Epworth Commentaries. London: Epworth, 1993.

Searle, John R. *The Construction of Social Reality.* London: Penguin, 1995.

————. *Expression and Meaning: Studies in the Theory of Speech Acts.* Cambridge: Cambridge University Press, 1979.

————. *Speech Acts: An Essay in the Philosophy of Language.* Cambridge: Cambridge University Press, 1969.

Seitz, Christopher R. *Isaiah 1–39.* Interpretation. Atlanta: John Knox, 1993.

Sheriffs, Deryck. *The Friendship of the Lord: An Old Testament Spirituality.* Carlisle: Paternoster, 1996.

Smart, James D. *The Strange Silence of the Bible in the Church.* London: SCM, 1970.

Soggin, J. Alberto. *Israel in the Biblical Period: Institutions, Festivals, Ceremonies, Rituals.* London: T. & T. Clark, 2001.

Theissen, Gerd. *The Shadow of the Galilean: The Quest of the Historical Jesus in Narrative Form.* London: SCM, 1987.

Thiselton, Anthony C. "Authority and Hermeneutics: Some Proposals for a More Creative Agenda." In *A Pathway into the Holy Scripture,* edited by Philip E. Satterthwaite and David F. Wright, 107–41. Grand Rapids: Eerdmans, 1994.

————. "Communicative Action and Promise in Interdisciplinary, Biblical, and Theological Hermeneutics." In *The Promise of Hermeneutics,* by Roger Lundin et al., 133–239. Grand Rapids: Eerdmans, 1999.

————. *The Two Horizons: New Testament Hermeneutics and Philosophical Description.* Exeter: Paternoster, 1980.

Thompson, Leonard L. *The Book of Revelation: Apocalypse and Empire.* New York: Oxford University Press, 1990.

Wainwright, Geoffrey. "The Language of Worship." In *The Study of Liturgy,* edited by Cheslyn Jones et al., 519–28. 1978. 2nd ed. SPCK, London 1992.

Watson, Francis. "Coleridge, S. T." In *A Dictionary of Biblical Interpretation,* edited by R. J. Coggins and J. L. Houlden, 124–25. London: SCM, 1990.

————. *Text, Church and World: Biblical Interpretation in Theological Perspective.* Edinburgh: T. & T. Clark, 1994.

Wink, Walter. *The Bible in Human Transformation: Toward a New Paradigm for Biblical Study.* Philadelphia: Fortress, 1973.

————. *Transforming Bible Study. A Leader's Guide.* 1980. 2nd ed. London: Mowbray, 1990.

Wright, N. T. *The Challenge of Jesus.* London: SPCK, 2000.

————. "How Can the Bible Be Authoritative?" *Vox Evangelica* 21 (1991) 7–32.

————. *Jesus and the Victory of God.* Christian Origins and the Question of God, vol. 2. London: SPCK, 1996.

————. "The Letter to the Romans." In *The New Interpreter's Bible,* edited by Leander E. Keck. 10:393–770. Nashville: Abingdon, 2002.

————. *Scripture and the Authority of God.* London: SPCK, 2005.

Scripture Index

Printed in Great Britain
by Amazon